Country Living

CHRISTMAS AT HOME

holiday decorating ✳ *crafts* ✳ *recipes*

Edited by Valerie Rains

HEARST
books

contents

introduction

WHAT MAKES A MERRY CHRISTMAS?

The proportions may vary from one home to the next, but the ingredients tend to hold true for most. To us, the jolliest holidays comprise a blend of the tried and true and the unexpected—beloved traditions along with whimsical surprises. Heirloom recipes, silly rituals, oddball ornaments, family in-jokes. Licking the beaters, baking breakfast bread, stringing a popcorn garland, and untangling the lights (okay, maybe not that one). Early pots of coffee and late-night sips of warm cocoa or mulled wine. They're about fun, magic, joy, and above all, the shedding of everyday preoccupations to be truly in the moment with the people you love best (or as many of them as you can fit under one roof).

Because there's always room for more holiday magic, we've mined the magazine's archives to bring you some of our favorite country-Christmas decorating ideas, handmade gift inspiration, and recipes for unbeatable entrees, elevated side dishes, and holiday desserts so pretty they belong on a pedestal.

As for the silly rituals and family in-jokes—well, those are still all up to you.

PART 7

decorate

IDEAS FOR EVERY ROOM

Decorating your home for the holidays is like unwrapping a gift in reverse: Instead of peeling back the layers of patterned paper, gleefully ripping off ribbons and bows (or gingerly removing them to store in a box for later use), you're adding on layers, bundling your home—and by extension, all those who enter it—in your most appealing, and personal, array of seasonal accoutrements. From the day you haul home that prized specimen from the tree farm (or unearth your beloved artificial number from the storage shed) to the moment the last heirloom linens have been laid out on the dining room table, prepping your home for another year of Christmas festivities is an act of celebration in and of itself.

The holidays are all about anticipation, and nothing sets the stage for the good times to come like a joyfully adorned front door. Seasonal greenery, a cheery bunting, wintry artwork, even a full-size tree—it's all fair game, indoors or out.

gather

WARM AND INVITING SPACES

From the tree adorned with one-of-a-kind ornaments amassed over many holidays past to the cherished mantelpiece mainstays that have become as much a part of your annual December ritual as tuning into the Weather Channel's televised Santa Tracker, so many of the cornerstones of holiday décor find a home in your family room and foyer. The most memorable setups are anything but cookie-cutter—they don't even have to be red and green! All they have to be is yours.

White walls and furniture provide a pristine backdrop for cheery pops of color and unexpected holiday accents—ice skate–inspired stockings, a cardboard taxidermy deer sporting a Rudolph-red clown nose—to really shine. Textured throw pillows and papier-mâché ornaments in red and blue keep things cozy, warming up the otherwise icy palette. It's an airy-meets-merry winter wonderland.

Festive First Impressions

Let the neighbors duke it out over who's got the
most elaborate light display. Winning the award for warmest welcome is a
much more worthwhile—and less electric bill–inflating—pursuit.

What better way to say joy to the world—okay, neighborhood—than a house embellished with barn red and evergreen? This outbuilding's classic L-arm exterior light fixtures add a touch of the latter hue year-round, while shedding light on a festive-meets-functional arrangement of everyday planters, pots, and pails piled high with birch logs, plus a pair of tiny trees bedecked with pinecones. But the greenery doesn't stop there: An all-weather wreath of Scotch pine and fir upgraded with LED lights and hardy ornaments complements a similarly adorned drape of greenery above.

Whether your guests have come from over the river and through the woods or just from the other side of the cul-de-sac, a rustic wreath (assembled from a twist of moss- and lichen-covered twigs), a stack of cozy plaid flannel blankets, and a vintage Danish muller filled with warm spiced wine will knock the chill right off.

Not the Santas and sleighbells type? Relying on subtler seasonal elements that can carry you from fall through the end of the year makes for a cozy compromise. Dress up a grapevine wreath (or a pair of them) by nesting nuts and apples in the lower half, then hang with 3-inch-wide burlap ribbon. Repurpose a bushel basket as a rustic planter for shrubbery or a mini tree, and display coordinating wool blankets on the rungs of a wooden ladder. The finishing touch: a stash of firewood stacked on a bench, which promises a crackling good time inside.

A pinecone wreath is another earthy way to get the holiday point across, without a lot of flashy (jingle) bells and whistles.

Propped against a wall at one end of the porch, a giant toboggan stands sentry to accept December guests (when it's not carrying a crowd of them, cheeks flushed with cold, down a snowy hill). A pair of skates dangling from the door reinforces the playful message.

Crisscrossed wooden skis bring a winter-sports vibe as the base of a wreath (just hang a vintage pair in an X shape, and add the seasonal greenery on top). Grain sack trees give racing stripes a rustic twist—and you can pin holiday cards to the surface for an easy display. Layer on Nordic motifs such as a woolen snowflake throw and Fair Isle–inspired wrapping papers for even more ski-chalet chic.

A front-hall console or side table can become the stage for a joyful holiday vignette—a bowl of ornaments here, vintage figurines there. Stash extra blankets and throws in a basket beneath for more warm-and-fuzzy feelings.

Opening Acts

x x x

Greenery, goodie bags, and gift stacks galore! Set the scene as soon as guests step in the door with decorations for the foyer, staircase, and more.

BRIGHT IDEA
Drape a folded throw or a wide woolen scarf over a side chair's seat to add an unexpected pop of a holiday hue.

Commission a spare chest of drawers to serve as a way station for gifts. Add greenery or a wintry bouquet to act as an anchor for the arrangement.

Don't save all the presents for Christmas Eve. Treat overnight guests to welcome gifts of candy and hot cocoa mix, bundled in coffee mugs. Hung from a garland-draped banister, they brighten guests' arrival and point the way to their temporary digs all at once.

Who needs needles? This bare-branched ivory tree is the ideal small-space solution for the decorator who wants to maintain a mostly monochrome palette and an airy entryway feel.

Coats can go in the closet. This time of year, why not turn over the workaday rack's prime real estate to a display of gift-stuffed stockings or a hanging fabric advent calendar? Round things out with coordinating cushions on a hallway bench nearby, or a pet bed with a swapped-out seasonal cover.

Cool Comforts

Not so into red and green? Cool and muted hues can still be plenty merry.
It's all about being true (blue) to your personal style.

Behind the stairs, tucked-away built-in seating and shelving offer a sweet nook for stashing extra gifts—or a convenient perch for arrivals to sit down and unpack them.

With its natural textures, calming palette, and glinting hints of sparkle, this easy-breezy stairwell is nautically nice. On the banister, a 2-inch-thick hemp rope accented with mercury-glass clamshell ornaments gives classic greens a shipshape look, while driftwood tabletop trees and a shell-encrusted sconce underscore the coastal theme.
Top watery-blue and sand-colored kraft paper packages with a seaside ornament for a little extra splash.

A vibrant green swag and golden beaded garland make a casually glam complement to this romantic, blue-hued hallway, while drawing the eye up to emphasize the room's lofty proportions.

Put It in Neutral

Subdued seasonal accents drawn from the natural world
embody an "all is calm, all is bright" approach to the holidays.

All the winter embellishments this midcentury modern-meets-country setting needs are a few well-placed pinecones and a none-too-flashy tree.

A diminutive potted evergreen straight out of the Charlie Brown playbook gets an extra dose of charm from a perky plaid bow tied around its upper trunk. The only other color in the room comes from a lush garland and a stack of snuggly blankets below.

Who says ornaments only belong on trees? In this library-like den, floor-to-ceiling built-in bookshelves glimmer with gold and silver baubles that play off the room's glass and brass accents.

A clubby-meets-campy vibe prevails in this deep teal–hued living room, thanks to a kitschy display of paint-by-numbers (scored at estate sales), a taxidermy deer head with ornament-adorned antlers, grain-sack stockings, and an impressive collection of 4-H ribbons (sourced, en masse, from a thrift store's dollar bin), hung alongside ornaments on the tree.

Vibrant Living Rooms

xxx

From Santa's big down-the-chimney entrance to all that exhilarating unwrapping, this is the space where so much holiday magic happens. And getting it ready is half the fun.

Antique ornament fans know: Vintage Shiny Brite® balls are a go-to for adding color to a holiday scheme.

Dress a mantelpiece with evergreens in contrasting textures for a more organic-looking arrangement.

the perfect winter fire

Whether you're playing a game of charades or simply warming yourself after a bracing winter walk, there are few things nicer than a crackling open fire at this time of year. Here's how to get the warmest glow.

GREEN OR SEASONED?

Like a good wine, firewood improves when stored and matured correctly. Recently chopped, or "green," wood is still full of water. It will burn less efficiently and smolder, potentially causing a dangerous buildup of creosote in the flue that could lead to chimney fires. Cutting and splitting wood, and keeping it under cover in a well-ventilated store—known as seasoning—allows the moisture to escape. As a general rule, hardwoods take two to three years to season, while softwoods take a year.

SOFTWOOD OR HARDWOOD?

Hardwoods (such as oak) have a greater density of fibers than softwoods (such as pine), so they provide you with more fuel, which burns longer and slower than the same volume of softer logs. However, seasoned softwoods create more intense flames, which are useful for getting a fire going.

WHICH TREE?

Different types of tree burn in different ways, so experiment to find the one that best suits your requirements:

* **ASH** is considered to be the best firewood, as it will burn evenly without being seasoned.

* **OAK** takes at least two years to season, but it's worth the wait: It makes excellent firewood, burning slowly and producing lots of heat.

* **PINE** and **LARCH** blast out plenty of heat when seasoned but have a tendency to spit, so they are best used in a wood stove. Pine twigs are also great for starting a fire.

* **APPLE** and **PEAR** will scent the room with a glorious aroma and are good for cooking over, as the smoke gives a lovely flavor to food.

Equal parts glitzy and grounded, this scene gives everyday elements extra-special upgrades: Brass fruit votives shed light on a deer with gilded antlers, and gleaming metal leaves peek out among pine needles. Paper flowers and greenery sprigs seem almost sculptural when displayed under glass.

This neutral, understated home's reclaimed-beam mantel finds a fitting complement in a swag of green and brown magnolia leaves. The round, driftwood-framed mirror above reflects light and stands in for a wreath.

A limited—but warm and tactile—palette of natural materials (leather, wood, ceramic, and stone) defines this minimalist, yet still cozy, home. An unfussy asymmetric wreath leaves room for negative space above the fireplace.

Filled with split logs (some accented with tinted chalk for extra panache), a nonworking fireplace still provides a festive focal point for this family room.

An old vintage star light sourced at a flea market brings carnival flash to this Christmassy mantel.

HOW TO ADD

a little santa magic

MAKE CHRISTMAS MORNING MORE MEMORABLE with snowprints left by Santa. Simply trace a pair of men's boots or dress shoes on cardboard. Cut out the template and place it by the fireplace or front door and sprinkle powdered sugar around the edges. Remove cardboard, being careful to keep outline of shoe intact. Ta-da! Hard (and fast!) proof that Santa Claus has been to town.

It doesn't have quite the carrying capacity of Santa's sleigh, but a vintage wooden wheelbarrow can still do a bang-up job of holding (or hauling) piles of presents.

Holiday-appropriate plaid accents, like the throw on the ladder and the scarf on the caribou, add timeless (and lighthearted) charm to this family room. Displayed year-round, apothecary bottles bring typographic punch to the mantel and make handy holders for individual evergreen sprigs. ▶

Embrace Antique Touches

Vintage decor (whether originally intended for the holidays or not) adds serious charm to a seasonal scene. Figurines and furniture, stockings and signage—the possibilities are endless (sort of like Santa's to-do list).

In this pattern-packed living room, more is most definitely merrier.
Striped and plaid stockings play nicely under a painted-wood
rendering of Old Glory, and animal-adorned throw pillows make
themselves at home on quilt-covered armchairs. A lamp with a
map-printed shade and checked curtains amplify the ambience.

An antique mantel from the early 1900s frames this family room's nostalgic holiday details: old-timey stockings, throwback artwork, and a humble, natural evergreen swag. Kraft paper packages brightened with red and white string complement the classic aesthetic.

Need motivation to get a jump-start on gift wrapping? Small packages covered in vintage papers and tossed in a wooden bowl make for a happy tabletop display before the Big Day.
▼

Traditional Swedish Dala horses stand in festive formation atop a hand-me-down butternut dresser and an antique oval Shaker box. Above, an evergreen array of family photos are displayed.

Why stop at an evergreen swag when you can brighten your banister with colorful vintage ornaments and a big red bow to boot? A potted tree in a vintage potato chip can offers guests a subtle signal to drop any gifts on arrival, leaving their hands free to receive a cup of hot cocoa (or a hot toddy) straightaway.

Plaid fabrics and printed gift wrap deliver warmth and energy to this masculine, woodsy room, while bold red camping lanterns enliven the stone fireplace. A modestly sized Christmas tree gets a boost from a rustic wooden crate in the corner.

File this idea away for next year: An antique card catalog cabinet can provide an extra display area for extended family members' stockings or can be a great alternative if you don't have a mantel—and there's no end to the fun surprises you can stash in its drawers for curious visitors to discover.

Savor the Moment

A TRIP TO THE TREE FARM

SAY WHAT YOU WILL about the convenience of an artificial tree, but there's nothing like holiday decorating from the ground up. So go on a hot cider–fueled pursuit of this year's specimen. As is true for most family outings, good-natured arguments will ensue, but all will be forgiven by the time that slightly off-kilter fir finds its home. And as you go to hang that clay handprint ornament from 1972, you'll be reminded that family, like that one-of-a-kind tree and its humble homemade trimmings, is perfect in its imperfection. Take that, plastic.

Christmas Collectibles
Vintage Ornaments

These candy-colored retro trimmings will infuse your tree with the spirit of Christmases past. Here's what to look for:

1 INDENT: Originally designed to catch and reflect the candlelight of Victorian Christmas trees, fancy indented shapes had a resurgence in the 1950s. (They fell out of favor the following decade, when more subdued looks became popular.)

2 GLASS: The first glass ornaments were made in Germany in the 1800s; midcentury styles from Shiny Brite, the world's largest ornament company at that time, were originally sold at Woolworth's for as little as two cents for six and are still popular today.

3 CARDBOARD CAP: World War II rationing restricted the use of metal, so ornaments made during that period have now-coveted cardboard caps and string hangers. They also featured simpler designs, lacking the shiny "silvered" interior of prewar glass bulbs.

4 DIORAMA: Made in Europe and Japan, these ornaments display festive holiday scenes. Italian varieties such as the deer and elf vignette shown here command the highest prices.

5 COTTON: Constructed from cotton batting, this style, popular from the 1890s to the 1920s, is virtually unbreakable and was often given to children for decoration and play. Pieces from the noted firm Heubach are some of the most desirable finds.

6 DRESDEN: These embossed paper pieces derive their name from the German city in which they were crafted. Dresdens were fabricated from the 1880s to the 1910s; production ceased when the town was bombed during World War I. Due to their scarcity and extremely delicate materials, they are the most expensive ornaments on the market. With its elaborate tack and gilded florets, the pictured horse head is a prime example.

A limited palette of silver, blue, and white brings cohesion to this snowflake-centric tree, while beneath its boughs a colorful Christmas village nestled atop faux sheepskin rugs makes for a cool alternative to the standard gift display.

Tree Styles

× × ×

Your family's Christmas tree is as unique as a fingerprint—or a time capsule—
embodying decades of DIY experiments, family memories and milestones,
and evolving addresses and tastes. But that doesn't mean
you can't take creative cues from other well-executed specimens.
Here are a few noteworthy examples from across the aesthetic spectrum.

Overflowing with good tidings, this homespun tree trades glittering tinsel for an assortment of holiday greeting cards (clipped to jute rope with mini clothespins), and a spirited mix of jewel-toned ornaments from the 1950s and '60s.

RETHINK
the tree skirt

There's more than one way to spruce up a trunk. Here, five ideas for trees big and small:

1. A woven bushel basket lends rustic appeal (position it under a potted tree right side up, or cut a hole in the bottom and invert it over a larger tree's stand).

2. A no-nonsense galvanized bucket conjures farmhouse charm beneath a pine or fir.

3. Slipped over a potted tree's planter, a burlap coffee sack perks things up.

4. Repurpose a vintage food storage tin (printed with advertisements for bygone brands) to hold a tabletop tree.

5. Arrange a few affordable sheepskin throws around a larger tree's base to approximate a snowy scene.

Featuring jolly red lettering, this former potato chip pail is the perfect vessel for a mini tree.

Dried citrus wheels and kumquat danglers infuse this tree with sunshine (and scent); gingerbread snowflakes provide their wintry counterpart.

◀ Even a petite tree, when
dressed up with antique
glass balls, artificial
birds, and lifelike berries,
can provide all the
evergreen appeal of a
full-size specimen. Just
perch it atop a spare
chair and surround
with seasonal accents
for eye-level impact.

BRIGHT IDEA
Assign each family member a sled, and pile on gifts accordingly.

Burlap poinsettias, a seven-pointed paper star crafted from vintage sheet music, and a cascade of bells attached to jute webbing strike a charming and rustic note, while antique sleds double as throwback decor elements and clever gift-delivery systems.

A tree embellished with pennants from national parks and roadside attractions offers a ready source of conversation starters and ample opportunities for reminiscing about family adventures past.

Wintry woodland frills (owl and deer ornaments; a forest of flocked bottle-brush trees in lieu of a skirt) evoke a snow-laden trek to grandmother's house, while flickering clip-on, battery-operated candles hark back to the days of lighting tapers in windows nightly. Antique snowshoes and skis reinforce the frosty feel.

The Great Outdoors

Your home's exterior provides even more opportunities for decor—
here are ideas for seasonal accents that carry the merry far beyond your front door.

Even outdoor (and in-between) spaces become vital sites for overflow activities when relatives arrive en masse. Here, woven chairs, a metal table, and a mounted stag turn an enclosed porch into a (wild) game room, in more ways than one.

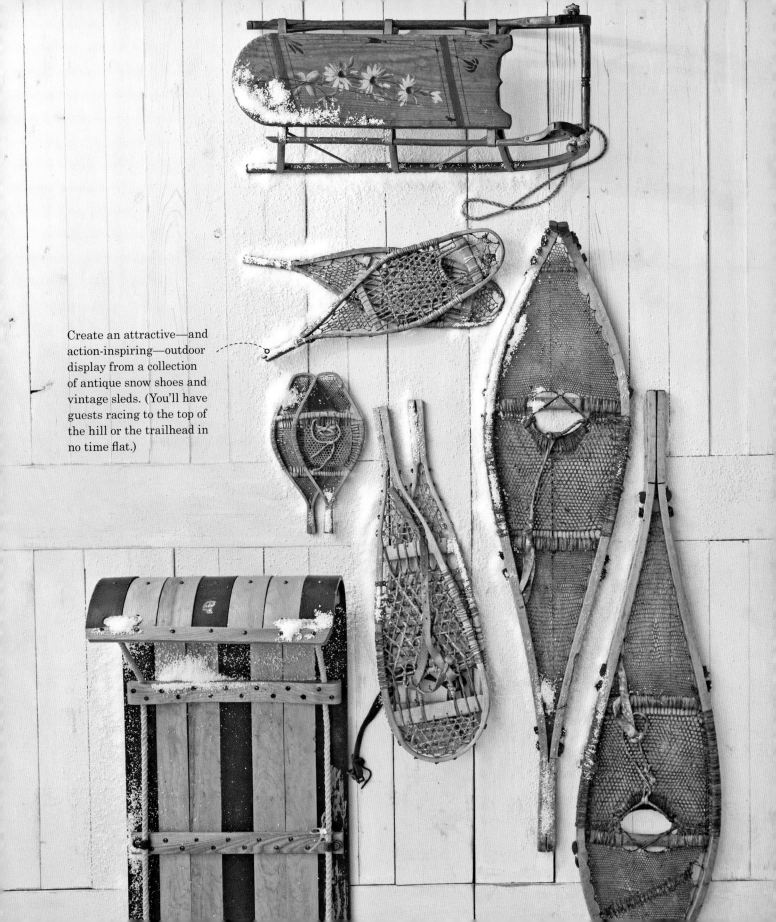

Create an attractive—and action-inspiring—outdoor display from a collection of antique snow shoes and vintage sleds. (You'll have guests racing to the top of the hill or the trailhead in no time flat.)

It's hard to say which adds more warmth to this outdoor scene— the blaze flickering in the fire pit, the cheery lanterns encircling the patio, blankets and throws awaiting use on each chair, or the extra-large Christmas tree gleaming through the picture window beneath a star-shaped twist of string lights.

Leaned against
a little-used vehicle,
an antique wooden sled
with a wintry all-white
wreath winks at
guests on their way
in or out.

feast

INSPIRING SETTINGS FOR MEMORABLE MEALS

— — — — — — — — — —

If we're being honest, our dining rooms (and our kitchens) see more action the last two months of the year than they do the other 10 months combined— or at least it feels like it. So shouldn't they be every bit as inviting as the rest of the house? Break out the mini wreaths and the festive ribbon—it's time to cook up some Christmas spirit.

Merry red ribbons look even more lively in an otherwise subdued dining room like this one, while a weathered wood crate centerpiece brings good tidings to the table.

Christmassy Kitchens

Cooking for the holidays is often a communal experience. A few seasonal upgrades will add sugar and spice to the old chop-stir-roll-gab-repeat routine—for you and your hands-on helpers.

Make kitchen lingerers more comfy with a self-serve hot-drinks station. Here, an old biscuit display serves up fixins for cocoa, coffee, and tea.

Check out these seats: With a quick stitch-up job, old flannel shirts in red, black, and white plaid become bespoke seasonal toppers for standard industrial metal stools.

In an open-plan kitchen, it's easy to capitalize on the decorative touches in adjacent areas, like this cheery peek at a green and gold staircase garland that plays off the kitchen's shiny brass lamp and potted herbs.

Cedar branches, secured with invisible fishing line, curve naturally over a rounded pendant in this nook off the kitchen, while a cluster of pine cones adds another textural touch. A clutch of evergreen sprigs in a low ceramic vase bridges the two spaces.

Cheerful red serving ware and casual pops of greenery in unexpected vessels (mugs, ice buckets) give this camp-themed kitchen a Christmassy twist. (Even the wreath in the window hangs from a strap of preppy plaid fabric.)

OPEN FOR

BRIGHT IDEA
Repurpose gingham tablecloths into curtains with a few drapery clips.

Savor the Moment
DISH DUTY

ANY OTHER TIME OF THE YEAR, washing dishes can feel like the most tedious chore. And when you see the stack of plates and cheese-crusted casserole dishes after one of the biggest meals of the year, it's natural to want to get the heck out of Dodge. But this postprandial ceremony offers the perfect opportunity to spend some quality time, elbow-to-elbow, with your favorite relative at the sink. As the rest of the family retires to watch *It's a Wonderful Life* (for the 47th time) or heads outside for a walk, dish duty becomes a quietly intimate moment. You're left alone, busy with mindless work, and free to talk in-depth about the family history you're a little foggy on, or to get the real scoop on that boy who broke your niece's heart. (Jerk.) Wash. Dry. Put away. It's essentially a free therapy session where your outlook—and glassware—becomes crystal clear. And you can rest assured you won't be interrupted, because there's no way anyone is going to accidentally wander in to help do the dishes.

Bursts of Christmas cheer can come from just about anywhere: a pair of cherry-red task lights over the kitchen counter, a red-and-white floor runner, a checked hand towel hanging from the stove, or salvaged vintage metal signage from long-gone candy companies or tree farms. The best part? Each element offers a clear nod to the holidays without feeling too theme-y.

Why not enliven a compact dining nook with a pair of (practically) pint-size trees? Just make sure they're not so tall that they block seated diners' views. ▶

All-white-and-wood spaces lend themselves well to simple moments of seasonal color—say, a collection of tomato-hued cookware set out on display, mix-and-match country linens in apple red, and a bouquet of berry-bright blossoms on the tabletop.

BRIGHT IDEA
Swap out the standard apples and bananas for a shiny pile of metallic ornaments in your fruit bowl.

Lush, full swags call attention to this mint-colored kitchen's generously sized windows, cultivating a casually festive atmosphere; the sink-side mini tree serves as an evergreen exclamation point. ▼

◀ There's hardly a spot in the house that can't be made merrier with a few well-placed wreaths and boughs. This streamlined cook space's windows show off a trio of understated circles, connected by an elegant black ribbon that suits the gallery-like room's overall style and echoes the black fireclay sink below.

A wall-spanning hutch acts as the functional focal point for this festive dining room.

▲

Dress up open dish storage with lengths of mixed greenery—a reminder to make every meal, not just the big, multicourse ones, merry.

Even a wood-sheathed stove hood can harbor a holiday flourish, accented with (unmeltable) faux frost.

Savor the Moment THE HOMETOWN GROCERY STORE RUN

THE NIGHT BEFORE CHRISTMAS may be better known for visions of sugarplums, but shoppers in pursuit of last-minute grocery staples only have eyes for that one forgotten ingredient that sets Grandma's stuffing recipe apart from the rest. And while the mad, beat-down-the-doors scramble for water chestnuts—or that last can of Libby's® canned pumpkin—is not particularly glamorous, there is something beautiful about unexpected run-ins with long-lost acquaintances—the childhood friend you haven't seen in years, the high school English teacher who coached you through *Beowulf*, or the sweet church organist who asks if you're still playing the piano. You emerge from the chaos with both the canned pumpkin and a sense of gratitude for people who, after all these years, still remember you—even if they forgot to buy water chestnuts. Turns out Memory Lane can be found on aisle 3.

On Display

4 Tabletop Traditions

All right, ironstone addicts and jadeite fiends: This is the time when your collection obsession earns its keep (and its cupboard space). Not invested yet? Consider adding these country classics to your antiques show shopping list.

| № 1 |

Transferware

In the 1700s, the emerging British middle class desired an affordable alternative to delicate hand-painted tableware. Pottery factories in Staffordshire, England (think Spode and Wedgwood), responded with transferware, and by the end of the century, thousands of mass-produced pieces were getting their signature ornate look by transferring a printed pattern from a copper plate to a special paper, and then to the earthenware.

DISPLAY TIP
Glass-front cabinets give a jewel-box effect to Pyrex® pieces. Add a wreath with bright ornaments for extra punch.

| № 2 | ### Pyrex

More festive than formal, rainbow-hued Pyrex platters, bowls, and casseroles have long topped color-loving collectors' lists. The durable cookware line, developed in 1915 for use in science labs and kitchens, has attracted a new generation of fans of late, who are drawn to its charming silkscreened patterns and vibrant tones—the brighter, the better.

| № **3** |

Ironstone

Named for its durability, this glazed earthenware was originally manufactured in Staffordshire, England, in the early 19th century, and comes in a wide variety of shapes and sizes, from stately platters to hardy casserole dishes. (Its milky shade provides the perfect quiet backdrop for vibrant cranberry red, sweet-potato orange, and the other delightful hues of a typical holiday feast.) British manufacturers to look for include Church Gresley Pottery, Hartshorne Pottery, Spode, and Waterloo Pottery. Also consider pieces by U.S. makers like Lenox, Homer Laughlin, and Onondaga Pottery.

DISPLAY TIP A dark backdrop lends striking contrast to the monochromatic collection.

№ 4 | Jadeite

Developed during the Great Depression as a way to reuse green scrap glass, jadeite became a big seller in the post–World War II boom years and is still prized among collectors today. Look for logos from the three original jadeite purveyors—McKee, Jeannette, and Anchor Hocking (whose items are labeled Fire King)—to ensure authenticity.

Bunches of bay leaves and decorative stars hanging in the windows give this dining room a romantic cottage vibe.

Family-Style Feasts

Here are some appealing ideas for creating a celebratory tablescape, whether you're gathering everyone in a formal dining room or assembling an archipelago of dining surfaces to accommodate a sprawling brood.

Colorful streamers, mercury-glass pine cones, and a flurry of honeycomb-paper snowflakes suspended above this dining table bestow an ebullient atmosphere for the big meal.

HOW TO SET

a festive (not fussy) tablescape

Feast your eyes on these essentials
for a warm and welcoming spread.

❶ START WITH SIMPLE GREENERY. Look no farther
than your backyard for the makings of a pretty
table runner. Wood slices add a rough-hewn touch
and can also log time as chargers or makeshift
cake stands.

❷ ADD A POP OF PLAID. A classic tartan tablecloth
dresses up a space in a polished (but not
pretentious) way.

❸ TRY SOMETHING NEW. Splurge on one or two
special touches for the table, whether it's a fancy
set of double old-fashioned glasses or hand-thrown
ceramic dinner plates.

❹ INCORPORATE SOMETHING OLD. For a whimsical
place setting, slide handwritten name cards into the
slots of vintage sleigh bells and give new meaning
to "be there with bells on."

❺ CAST A ROSY GLOW. Candles in oversize mason jars
and frosted bulb lights add instant ambience. Rose-
gold flatware, a striking alternative to silver, warms
things up even more.

Consider this the perfectly imperfect holiday table: Set with mismatched plates, linens, and silver collected over time, it is, quite fittingly, as beautifully hodgepodge as the people who will soon surround it. Personalize the place settings with old family photos to help guests find their seats—and to inspire "remember when" banter.

In an all-neutral dining room like this one, a little holiday nostalgia goes a long way. Here, a snow-spritzed fiberglass bell that once hung in a 1950s department store makes the breakfast table the perfect spot to ring in Christmas morning.

Sophisticated year-round displays (vintage black-and-white high school class photos, an impressive ironstone collection) are seasoned with not-so-serious accents such as Putz houses, bottle brush trees, and Santa mugs.

easy kraft paper place settings

FOUR WAYS

All you really need is a roll of kraft paper and minimal DIY skills to transform your dining table just in time for Christmas dinner. Bonus: No cranberry-stained table linens!

① FOR A SIMPLE, MODERN LOOK, use a pencil to lightly draw three sides of a 16-inch square, leaving the top side open. Write a guest's name in the center of the open space, extending the lines on either side of the name to complete the square. Trace over the pencil lines with a white paint marker and allow to dry. This tablescape compliments materials like marble and metallic linens.

② FOR WOODSY, RUSTIC CHARM, layer a birch bark sheet (sold in craft supply stores) atop a kraft paper runner with a hand-tied whip-stitched edge (made using a hole punch and contrast-colored twine). Pair with gingham and wood accents and outdoorsy place card holders.

③ TO MAKE A BASKET-WEAVE MAT for the center of the runner, cut an 18-inch-wide by 24-inch-long piece of kraft paper. Draw 1-inch lines along the width of the paper, leaving a 1-inch border on the narrow ends and a ½-inch border on the long sides. Use a utility knife and ruler to cut along the lines. Thread 30 (½-inch by 23-inch) strips of paper through the lines in a basket-weave pattern. Secure the ends with tape and cut off the excess, then position the woven mat atop the center of a plain paper runner. Along with the woven mat, rose-gold flatware and earthy, clay-rimmed dinner plates use textures and finishes to elevated effect.

④ A SWEETLY PRETTY LOOK IS EASY TO ACHIEVE: Just use a craft punch to add a lace-like edge along the paper runner and choose dinnerware that creates a bouquet of complementary botanical-inspired prints. Finish with a floral napkin tied with a ribbon, a decorative place card, and a floral sprig.

NOTE
Each of these DIY designs begins with an 18-inch-wide kraft paper runner, cut to your desired length.

Casually elegant elements like pale blue dinnerware, tiny fairy lights, and shimmering crinkled fabric add up to an enchanting—but still approachable—place setting.

Craft an enduring keepsake by making reprints of old family photos and gluing them onto a piece of cardstock. Embellish with a vintage button and a length of lace, and inscribe the year and the day's menu on the reverse.

Surrounded by white walls and gleaming brass fixtures, this handsome, down-to-earth farmhouse table takes on a starring role. With so few decorative distractions, a simple wreath hung from a ribbon is enough to say, "It's Christmastime."

HOW TO SET UP

5 made-to-order mini bars

Establishing a self-service drinks station and stocking it thoughtfully saves everyone time (and trips to the kitchen) in the holiday season.

BRIGHT IDEA
Clip affordable plaid flannel sheets to a curtain rod for quick-change seasonal window coverings.

| № 1 |

CHOOSING A BAR WITH AMPLE STORAGE for glassware and bottles leaves room for a cheery vase of branches or blooms on the drink-mixing surface. This one is actually an old typesetter's stand topped with marble.

| №2 | **NOT A BIG TIPPLER?** A minimal setup—a couple bottles of wine, one nice whiskey—atop a sideboard, cabinet, or console still makes an elegant offering for guests.

| №3 | **SHORT ON ICE BUCKETS** (or space in the fridge)? A cement planter can serve as a sturdy secondary chiller for cider or champagne.

| №4 | **A LONG LOWER SHELF** frees up this console's surface for muddling and mixing, while a woven basket corrals the rest of the bottles below.

| №5 | **A WHEELED BAR CART** creates an extra surface for both drinks and gifts and can easily be relocated when not in use.

Moving a holiday meal from the formal dining room to a more laid-back space might be just the ticket for your fun-loving family. Here, thick wool blankets soften the seating at this wooden table and bench, and a red and white checked table runner transports the simple pleasures of a summer picnic to a holiday setting.

ODE TO THE
All-Grown-Up Kids Table

YOU MAY HAVE GRADUATED TO THE "BIG" TABLE decades ago, but somehow being around family puts us back in the roles of our youth. You, your siblings, and your cousins might have kids of your own, or you may run a company or be a best-selling novelist, but when the family breaks bread together, you will always be the girl who spent her beach vacation in headgear. Inevitably, someone will try to make you laugh during the blessing. But with all of the responsibilities of adulthood, it's nice to know there's one place where you will always be a kid, and where a cousin knows just how to get your goat—no matter how big you get.

dream

COZY SLEEPING QUARTERS

Santa's working around the clock these days—and so can your Christmas decor. Keep the holiday spirit going 24 hours a day with joyful adornments even in the bedrooms. (How else are you going to ensure that visions of sugarplums dance in their heads?)

Bold buffalo-check bedding and a king-size garland give this master bedroom plenty of holiday oomph.

Blanket Statements

× × ×

Swapping seasonal bedding in for the winter months is a quick and easy way to warm up a room—whether you opt for peekaboo poinsettia-red bed sheets, heirloom quilts with holiday motifs, or piles of pillows in mix-and-match snowflake-print shams.

A pop of red bed sheets—hidden under a duvet by day—serves as a nightly reminder that Santa Claus is coming soon.

A classic red lantern stationed atop a bedside tree stump makes the perfect (campy) complement to this sleeping loft's woolen blankets (not to mention that cheeky Teddy Roosevelt pillow).

Vintage Woolrich blankets and tartan pillow shams give this guest room a winter refresh, and a faux flokati rug adds a layer of softness underfoot. (Don't forget an evergreen branch on the bedside table!)

HOW TO CRAFT

a patchwork console skirt

Here's a super simple way to bring new life to a timeworn quilt that's been relegated to the cedar chest for good.

1 **LAY THE QUILT FLAT** and cut it into two halves down the vertical center.

2 **FIND AND MARK THE CENTER FRONT** of a simple console table. Starting from the marked point and working out to the left, use a staple gun to attach the cut edge of one piece to the top of the table, with the quilt's finished edge hanging down the center. Repeat with the second piece on the right side, leaving a small opening between the two finished edges. Trim excess quilt material.

3 **AT THE CENTER OF THE TABLE,** use a staple gun to attach one strip of excess material to the underside of the tabletop. (This will create the look of a pleat behind the gap between two pieces.)

4 **TOP THE TABLE** with a stained piece of wood to cover the exposed staples.

BRIGHT IDEA
A vintage cooler makes for a clever lamp base.

◀ A red iron bed frame bolsters this room's seasonal palette, brought to life with layers of plaid, striped, and checked bedding and topped with a richly hued quilt.

Stored in a vintage glass-front cabinet painted a soft red, holiday linens are part of the decor even when they're not actively in use. ▶

Not interested in a whole-bed overhaul? A few Santa-themed pillows and warm faux fur throws make this kids' room December-ready. Garland-wrapped headboards, a small Santa statue, and a pinwheel of vintage state park flags round out the nostalgic scene.

BRIGHT IDEA
This homeowner repurposed the ends of an antique daybed to create a matched pair of headboards.

Low-effort, high-impact additions like red pillows, a crimson-covered book, and a potted mini tree are surefire ways to prep bedrooms for the holidays. The Federal-style mirror above this bed is a perfect stand-in for a wreath—just add ribbon.

Dreamy Garlands, Wreaths, and Trees

Bring the cornerstones of holiday decor into every nook of your home with scaled-down accents for all spaces.

In this master bedroom, cedar and princess pine come together in a fan shape, finished with a pinecone garnish for a fresh, unexpected accent. (The stems are wrapped together with floral wire and then attached to the wall with fishing wire and a temporary adhesive hook.)

"Planted" in a glazed bucket and strewn with pinecones and ribbon, this sophisticated feather tree creates a one-of-a-kind welcome in a guest room. A nearby bowl holds papier-mâché ornaments in primary hues.

Perfect for a kids' room, this retro tree is as jolly as Kris Kringle himself, thanks to a vintage tree stand and old-school ornaments.

There's nothing wrong with going all out in a bedroom—loads of patterned bedding, a decorated wreath, and a nearly full-size tree—if you've got the space to fill.

BRIGHT IDEA
Old Swiss Army blankets make great window coverings thanks to the weatherproof wool.

A vintage life preserver does double duty as a wreath with fresh greenery and a rope bow. Braided rag rugs and an array of Beacon and Pendleton blankets drive home the summer-camp-meets-winter-break aesthetic.

A pennant-bedecked potted tree directs guests' attention to the fully stocked games cabinet—handy for filling the sleepless hours before Santa's arrival.

▼

Stage a Nook or Two for Napping

x x x

It's no substitute for a guest bedroom, but when the postprandial slowdown overcomes your crowd, a few spots to catch some quick *z*'s will be appreciated by everyone on the premises.

A cot may be better for a catnap than an all-nighter, but with enough comfy pillows, the pop-up perch provides a solid place to take five. In the background, a pair of water skis becomes a Christmas tree with the help of lights and a star.

Unfurled for comfort atop a cot or employed as makeshift seating for movie night (*How the Grinch Stole Christmas,* anyone?), holiday-themed sleeping bags easily qualify as guest-bedroom MVPs.

Equipped with a pillow and tucked
away in a quiet corner, a spare
hammock comes in handy for a quick
nap before the next round.

FURNITURE.

When all the cousins, aunts, and uncles are in town, there's not going to be that much sleeping happening anyway. Indulge the excitement of a Christmas staycation with "campouts" by the tree and a s'mores party around the fire. All you need are a few fluffy sleeping bags, several spare pillows, and a high tolerance for cookie-fueled Christmas Eve high jinks.

give

GIFTS TO MAKE, BAKE, AND TAKE

These days, you can knock out half your holiday gift shopping (and most of your grocery list, to boot) on your smartphone while waiting in line for the pumpkin-spiked beverage du jour. But that only makes a handmade gift (or a perfectly imperfect farmstand gourd) that much more glorious. Put a little handmade magic back into the holiday with easy, one-of-a-kind gifts that don't require a PhD in papier-mâché; clever decor DIYs you won't see at every other open house on the block; and giftable baked goods that put packaged sweets to shame. Set down your cell phone—it's time to get creative.

What makes this tree so jolly and bright? An array of handmade ornaments in blue, red, and white. See pages 174–181 for the how-tos.

make

THOUGHTFUL GIFTS CRAFTED WITH CARE

Gadgets and gift cards have their place at the holidays, but they shouldn't be the only things filling the space beneath your tree. Make this year's gift exchange a little more memorable for everyone involved with handmade presents that show them you really know them.

From the first inkling of an idea to the very packaging you wrap it in, there are endless ways to infuse holiday gifts with meaning.

Gifts for the Sentimental Saver

You know the type—she never gets rid of anything she loves, no matter how chipped, frayed, or falling-apart-at-the-seams it may be. A thoughtful gift that cleverly repurposes a timeworn keepsake honors her preservationist impulse, while bringing a treasured item back into her regular rotation. (This is one present you can be sure won't be regifted next Christmas.)

TURN A BELOVED BLANKET
into a bolster pillow

1. Lay the quilt flat and cut two pieces measuring 36 inches wide by 22 inches high, being careful to center the quilt's primary pattern if desired.

2. Place the two pieces together, right sides facing in. Sew along the edges using a ½-inch seam, leaving a 5-inch opening at the center of a long edge (this is the bottom).

3. Turn cover right-side out, insert polyester fiberfill to desired fullness, and hand-stitch opening closed.

RETURN A SHRUNKEN SWEATER
to warming duty

1. Make a template, using card or paper, by drawing around your hot water bottle.

2. Add ¾ inch all around the pattern and cut it out.

3. Place this onto a single layer of a shrunken sweater or felted wool and cut it out. Mark this as A.

4. Place the template onto a second piece of wool, mark both bottom corners with pins or chalk, then add 6 inches extra in length and cut out. Mark as B.

5. Lay shape B on a table, and fold up the 6-inch edge, using pins or chalk on either side to keep it straight, so it's the same shape as the template.

6. Using some contrasting-colored wool thread, blanket stitch along the top edge of the fold.

7. Trim 1½ inches from the bottom edge of piece A.

8. Lay piece A on top of B, matching the top edges, and fold up the bottom of B to enclose the bottom of A. Pin all around.

9. Starting at the bottom right-hand corner, blanket stitch all around.

10. Slot your hot water bottle into the cover.

REFILL A MISMATCHED TEACUP
with a custom candle

1. Start with a pretty cup and saucer and some pre-waxed wicks. Thread the wick through the metal wick clip and cut it to the depth of the cup plus 2 inches.

2. Position the wick clip inside the cup at the center of the base, using a wick clip adhesive pad underneath and pressing firmly in place.

3. Wrap the end of the wick around a pencil and rest across the top of the cup to hold it upright.

4. Place wax pellets in a heatproof glass bowl over a saucepan of simmering water until melted. Add candle scent if desired at this stage, adjusting the strength to personal taste.

5. Carefully pour the wax into each cup to about ⅜ inch below the top and leave to set.

6. Once set, remove the pencil and trim the wick to ⅜ inch.

TRANSFORM A TEAPOT LID INTO A PHOTO HOLDER

Her daily pick-me-up will be twice as sweet thanks to a charmingly casual photo frame fashioned from an upcycled **teapot lid**. You can make it in minutes: Simply wrap **a 6-inch piece of artist's wire** around the lid's knob, leaving about 1 inch of excess at the end. Use **needle-nose pliers** to curl the remaining wire into a double loop and slide a cherished family photo between the loops.

CRAFT A NOVEL PLACEHOLDER FROM A TATTERED TOME

Dog-eared pages are one thing; a disintegrating cover or missing chapters are quite another. If your book club buddy is about to toss a read-to-death volume, deliver an unexpected plot twist in the form of this DIY gift. Using **a utility knife**, remove the book's spine, then line the inside with **patterned contact paper**. **Punch a hole** at the top and thread **twine** through.

CREATE PINCUSHIONS
with homespun charm

1. To construct the base of each pincushion, place the sharp side of a heart-shaped cookie cutter atop a thin piece of Styrofoam® (such as a produce tray from a grocery store). Press the cutter down to imprint the Styrofoam; then cut out the heart shape.

2. Cut a heart-shaped piece of fabric that's about ½ inch larger, all the way around, than the Styrofoam shape. Lay the fabric, right side down, on a flat surface and cover the back with Aleene's Tacky Glue®; then press the Styrofoam against the fabric. Pull the excess fabric up around the Styrofoam's edges and secure with more glue; let dry for 30 minutes.

3. Meanwhile, cut a square of fabric that's at least three inches larger, all the way around, than the cookie cutter. Hold the cutter, sharp side up, on your lap and lay the fabric right side down over the cutter. Push fiberfill stuffing into the cutter until the fabric protrudes about ¾ inch past the cutter, forming the pincushion. To close the cushion, fold over the remaining fabric and secure with a running stitch.

4. With the cushion still inside the cutter, cover the cushion's bottom with a generous coat of glue. Push the Styrofoam into the cutter so that it presses against the glue; hold in place for 3 minutes. Let dry for 30 minutes.

BRIGHT IDEA
Use iron-on fabric lettering to attach a name tag or initial to each bag.

TURN SENTIMENTAL TEXTILES
into practical, pretty totes

1. Start with a rectangle of printed cotton fabric (36 inches high by 13 inches wide for large bag; 28 inches high by 9 inches wide for small) and some cord (10 feet for large bag; 7 feet for small). With the right sides together, fold the fabric in half. With the fold at the bottom, stitch both side seams, using a ⅝-inch seam allowance and finishing the ends of the stitching securely. Leave a 1½-inch opening below the top edge on both side seams and a ¾-inch opening on the bottom of both sides for attaching the cord.

2. Press under ⅓ inch, then 1 inch around the top edge of the bag, and stitch to make a channel around the top rim for the cord. Turn the bag right side out.

3. Cut the cord in half. Use a safety pin to thread one piece through one side of the pocket at the top rim. Repeat with the second piece on the opposite side.

4. Thread and pin the ends of the cord inside the gaps at the bottom of both side seams. Turn the bag inside out and stitch in place securely. Turn the bag right side out and press.

ASSEMBLE A WALL-WORTHY MONOGRAM FROM VINTAGE SEWING SUPPLIES

Your craftiest friend or family member will appreciate this clever reuse of **old-fashioned thread spools** too pretty to throw out. Just cut her initial from a sheet of **thick cardboard** and **hot-glue spools** to the surface.

HOW TO ASSEMBLE

an organized wrapping station from upcycled finds

1 TURN BERRY BASKETS INTO BINS. Hung on adhesive plastic hooks, farmers' market produce baskets organize stamps, gift tags, and glitter, and free up counter space for wrapping packages.

2 COLLECT STICKERS, LABELS, AND STENCILS in a colorful compression coil.

3 USE FLOWER FROGS TO KEEP PAINT PENS and markers upright and within reach.

4 TURN A CHICKEN FEEDER INTO A SPOOL HOLDER. No need to keep your best-loved twine cooped up in a drawer. A chicken trough's feeder holes make a sweet roosting spot for these wrapping supplies. (This one's sitting atop a crate for extra height.)

5 EMPLOY WOODEN SPOONS AS RIBBON WRANGLERS. Hung with drapery rod brackets, this kitchen staple makes it easy to select the perfect shade (and unspool it without tangles).

6 TURN FISHING RODS INTO WRAPPING PAPER DISPENSERS. Use a handsaw to trim cane fishing poles (or any wooden pole) to desired lengths, then hang with drapery rod brackets.

A knotted leather hanging loop adds a touch of tactile appeal.

One-of-a-kind clock

Drill a hole in the center of **a round cutting board** and insert **clock hardware**. Attach vintage or industrial metal **number tags** with **black steel tacks**.

Gifts for the Kitchen Whiz

Say a hearty thank-you (and a subtle "seconds, please") to the skilled home cook who keeps you in rib-sticking casseroles and from-scratch desserts all season long with a DIY gift inspired by—or designed for use in—the kitchen.

Striped server

To give an oft-used **breadboard** store-in-plain-sight pizzazz, mark off lines on the back side of the board using varying widths of **painter's tape**; you can find it as thin as ⅛ inch and as wide as 6 inches. Apply **paint** and remove tape immediately. (**NOTE** To avoid direct contact between painted surface and food, we recommend decorating only one side of each board.)

BRIGHT IDEA
If decorating a whole set, alternate the orientations of the stripes for a more pleasing layered look.

BRIGHT IDEA
Don't forget the game
pieces! Add 12 to 16
1½-inch discs cut from
contrasting shades
of wood for an all-
around earthy
look.

Heirloom-worthy checkers set

Tape off a 64-square pattern with **painter's
tape** (you'll need at least a **16-inch-by-16-inch
board** to accommodate **standard checkers**),
then paint on squares with **acrylic paint**.

Smart spice rack

Use **screws** to attach **small wooden cheese boxes** to a **rectangular board**, making sure to leave enough clearance between rows for taller seasoning jars to come in and out. Add **a sturdy leather strap** for hanging.

Gifts for the Cozy Nester

Make his or her favorite place even more inviting with items that make the most of time spent at home or in the garden.

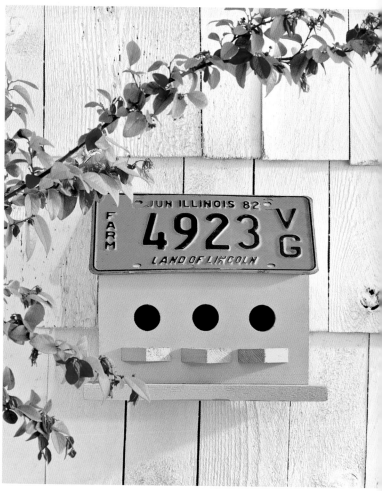

Cultivate a custom terrarium

Place 2 to 3 inches of **small gravel** (for drainage) in **a jar** followed by a couple inches of **soil**. Nestle in **hardy plants**—mini ferns and succulents both do well—and personalize with **trinkets** (toy deer, tiny houses) to add whimsy. **Water** as needed.

Remodel a basic birdhouse

Treat a bird-loving pal to a top-notch nesting spot finished with a **vintage license plate** (perhaps from her favorite place to go when she flies the coop). **Hot glue** or **screw** a plate to the top of an out-of-the-box **birdhouse** and **paint** the walls in a coordinating hue.

GARDEN-VARIETY UPGRADE
work gloves with floral fabric

1. Start with a pair of standard gardening gloves in her size. Measure the width of one glove opening and double it, adding ¾ inch (for a seam allowance). Cut a rectangle of paper to this measurement by 6 inches.

2. Lay the paper out with the short edges at the sides. Make three vertical cuts from the bottom to almost the top, evenly spaced across the width of the paper. Spread these out at the bottom so there are 1-inch gaps between each cut—this will create a flared shape. Pin this onto another piece of paper and cut out the shape to make a cuff template.

3. Draw and cut around the template four times from a piece of floral fabric.

4. Fold each fabric cuff in half, with the right sides together, and stitch the side using a ³⁄₁₆-inch seam allowance, pressing this open afterward.

5. Slip one cuff inside another with right sides together and stitch around the circumference of the wider end, using a ³⁄₁₆-inch seam allowance. Repeat for the other two pieces. Turn the right side out and press. You will end up with two double-sided cuffs.

6. Pin together the shorter edges of each individual cuff and neaten with a zigzag stitch. Remove the pins.

7. Pin each cuff to a glove and sew in place.

Craft a One-of-a-Kind Card

x x x

No disrespect to the printed family photo holiday mailer, but we bet some of your friends and relatives would appreciate a seasonal sentiment that's made from scratch. Here are three hands-on approaches.

... with a roller stamp

Use **latex paint** and a **patterned roller** with a festive design to produce original handmade cards. Cover the roller in an even amount of **paint** and practice your rolling technique on scrap paper a few times before printing your first card. (This idea also works well for enlivening plain wrapping paper, gift tags, and paper table runners.)

... with your thumb

All you need are a few **ink pads** and some plain **white note cards** to put your own stamp on these designs. To make seasonal greenery, press your thumbs into green ink to make leaves, then add berries and a bow with a **red marker** and stems with **green watercolor paint**. To make string lights, stamp thumbprints in a variety of **ink** shades onto the **paper**, and use a **black fine-tip marker** to draw a cord connecting the lights. To make a reindeer herd, stamp thumbprints in **brown ink** and press onto **a blank card**. Use **fine-tip markers** to draw antlers, eyes, and noses.

. . . with patterned paper

Cut out an ornament shape from **patterned paper** and back with **thin cardstock**. Thread **twine** through a hole at the top, tie in a bow, loop over the card, and secure.

The Little-Known History of
Holiday Cards

1843: Example of the first-known Christmas card

When Sir Henry Cole commissioned the artist John Callcott Horsley to design the first Christmas card, the concept was disapproved of by those who believed that its imagery wasn't in keeping with the season's religious focus. Nevertheless, a thousand were printed and then sold at his shop for one shilling each (a high price at the time). The tradition was born.

Raid the Craft Bin

The fabric and paper scraps and other little odds and ends that accumulate
in your crafts stash throughout the year can come in handy as unexpected trimmings
and unique gift wrap embellishments at holiday time.

An old mail
sorter, chock full
of cubbies and
compartments,
is an ideal place
to store and
organize all
manner of bits
and bobs.

Postage stamp gift tags

Make each gift a very special delivery with a gift tag decorated with a pretty **vintage stamp** featuring a holiday motif. Use steam from **a boiling kettle** to loosen the stamp from its old envelope (if it was attached to one), or just cut around its edges. Glue to **a plain gift tag** and add **brown twine, colorful string**, or **a ribbon** of your choice.

2 Stocking Stuffer Upgrades

Why not add a DIY mini gift to the standard assortments of sweets and silly trinkets?

| № 1 |

Use **metal snips** to create a durable monogram key keeper, making sure to sand down any sharp edges before dropping it in the sock.

| № 2 |

Glue a spool of thread to the top of a reusable **cork** for a wine stopper with style that won't quit.

Don't toss those too-small-for-a-gift-box **scraps of your prettiest wrap**. With a little **double-sided tape** it's easy to transform the paper into treat bags for small goodies or gift cards. Begin by **cutting** a rectangle of paper that's large enough to cover both sides of the item, plus a little extra. With the paper wrong side up, fold over a ½-inch flap on the long bottom edge and two short edges of the rectangle. Fold the paper in half along its longer side, wrong sides together, and use double-sided tape to stick together the flaps along the bottom and the side opposite the fold—this leaves the top open. Fold over ¾ inch at the top and cut the corners at an angle to make the envelope-style flap. Label with a slip of contrasting paper and seal with a **small sticker**.

To make smaller gifts extra special, **stamp** a snowflake design on **paper bags** and personalize with a **stencil**.

BRIGHT IDEA
Use these paper pouches to dress up individual cookies or other home-baked treats—just wrap each one in parchment paper or cellophane before inserting in the envelope.

Small Wonders

× × ×

Give little presents big impact with a smart packaging idea designed just for them.

Turn a **paper bag** into pretty packaging by using a decorative punch around the top edge. Stick **lace tape** along the bottom, fill, scrunch, and tie with **ribbon**.

A **matchbox** is just the right size for small gifts, such as dainty earrings, rings, and pins. Cover with contrasting **patterned papers** and fill with **bright tissue**.

Handmade Gift Wrap

Here are two equally charming strategies for designing your own.

THE EASY VERSION

make a grain sack–inspired stamp

1. Start with a 2-millimeter-thick sheet of craft foam and a rolling pin. Cut strips of foam in desired widths to simulate a grain sack's stripes.

2. Place two to three pieces of double-sided tape on one side of rolling pin. Secure one end of foam strip to tape and wrap around rolling pin. Trim end if needed and secure to tape.

3. Repeat process for other foam strips, cover with ink, and roll away!

Rolling Pin Stamp
3 Ways to Use It

Give paper goods a fresh spin with the help of this homemade crafting tool.

| № 1 |

Dress up your holiday-card envelopes or send post-holiday thank-you notes on a sweet striped stationery set.

| № 2 |

Put your stamp on an ordinary brown bag and drop small presents inside.

| № 3 |

Give plain old tags instant charm.

THE DELUXE VERSION
make moldable foam stamps

1. Start with a moldable foam stamp (available at craft stores), a raised inkpad in a similar size, and plain smooth paper for printing on. There are two ways to create images on moldable foam stamps: by drawing directly on them or taking an impression. If you do the latter, you'll be able to reuse them. You can also use both sides of the block.

2. To draw your own design, gently press a wooden skewer at a 20- or 30-degree angle (to avoid tearing) into the foam to create indentations—you may want to draw a light design in pencil first. To create dots, pierce the foam and rotate the wooden skewer.

3. To take an impression from a piece of lace (as seen here), make a design from cut sections and glue them to the cardboard (see top right).

Once dry, follow the instructions for the foam blocks—you will need to warm the side you want to make an impression on by holding it above a toaster or iron for about 15 seconds. (Do not let it come into contact with the source of heat or it will burn.) Press the block directly on top of the lace design and hold for a few seconds. If you make an error, warm the foam and start again.

4. To print a drawing or an impression, press the foam block onto the raised inkpad, making sure the image is evenly covered with ink, and then press onto the paper.

5. Experiment with printing in different colors and by staggering the design. You could also print gift tags and Christmas cards.

bake

SWEET GOODNESS TO SHARE

We bake to comfort, we bake to bond, but most of all, we bake to cheer and celebrate. And few gifts please so consistently as a home-baked treat—sweet, shareable, and undeniably made with care. Plus, they always fit—no matter how many other holiday indulgences may have preceded them (which is more than you can say for that snazzy new button-down).

Gifts from the kitchen are as fun to make as they are to receive, and the possibilities for elaboration on classic themes are endless. See ya later, same-old Christmas cookies. There's a new batch in town.

STRING LIGHT
SUGAR COOKIES

Try an assortment of crushed mint hard candies, rock candy, dragées, and M&M's® to add texture and color to the "bulbs." Shoestring licorice in a complementary hue stands in for wire.

MAKES *about 56 cookies*
WORKING TIME *1 hour, 30 minutes*
TOTAL TIME *2 hours, 30 minutes*

- 3 cups all-purpose flour, spooned and leveled, plus more for dusting
- ½ teaspoon kosher salt
- 1 cup (2 sticks) unsalted butter, at room temperature
- 2 ounces cream cheese, at room temperature
- 1 cup sugar
- 1 large egg
- 1 teaspoon pure almond extract
- ½ teaspoon pure vanilla extract
- ½ recipe White Vanilla Frosting (recipe follows)

   Candy: Blue, white, and green candy balls; crushed blue mint hard candies; silver and white dragées; mint M&M's; white sanding sugar; blue and green Sixlets®; crushed green and blue rock candy; white nonpareils; shoestring licorice

1. Whisk together the flour and salt. Beat the butter, cream cheese, and sugar with an electric mixer on medium speed until light and fluffy, 2 to 3 minutes. Beat in the egg and extracts. Gradually beat in the flour mixture until combined. Divide the dough in half, flatten into disks, and wrap in plastic wrap. Chill at least 1 hour.

2. Preheat the oven to 325°F. Line two baking sheets with parchment paper. On a floured surface, roll one disk of dough to ¼ inch thick. Cut cookies with a 3-inch light bulb–shaped cookie cutter. Make a hole in the top of each cookie with a skewer.

3. Bake until the edges are golden brown, 11 to 12 minutes. Cool on the pan for 5 minutes; remove to a wire rack to cool completely. Repeat with remaining dough. Reroll and cut scraps once.

4. Spread a thin layer of frosting on each cookie. Decorate with candy. Thread licorice through holes for the "wire."

WHITE VANILLA
FROSTING

MAKES *about 5 cups*
WORKING TIME *10 minutes*
TOTAL TIME *10 minutes*

2 cups (4 sticks) unsalted butter, at room temperature

6 cups sifted confectioners' sugar

1 teaspoon pure vanilla extract

Pinch kosher salt

1. Beat the butter with an electric mixer on medium speed until creamy, 1 to 2 minutes. Add the sugar, ½ cup at a time, beating well and scraping down the sides of the bowl after each addition. Beat in the vanilla and salt.

2. Store frosting in an airtight container at room temperature up to 2 days or in the fridge for 2 weeks.

GIFT-READY PRESENTATION
Line a berry basket with polka-dot tissue paper and add cookies. Wrap with rickrack, and sew the trim in place with a button and embroidery thread.

BISCUIT & JAM
COOKIES

MAKES *about 20 sandwich cookies*
WORKING TIME *30 minutes*
TOTAL TIME *1 hour, 30 minutes*

3½ cups plus 2 tablespoons cake flour, spooned and leveled, plus more for surface

½ cup sugar

½ cup packed light brown sugar

2 tablespoons baking powder

1 teaspoon baking soda

1 teaspoon kosher salt

1 cup (2 sticks) cold unsalted butter, cut up

1 cup large unsweetened coconut flakes

1 large egg

½ cup heavy cream

2 teaspoons raw sugar

½ cup strawberry jam

1. Preheat the oven to 425°F with racks in the upper and lower thirds. Line two baking sheets with parchment paper. Place the flour, sugar, brown sugar, baking powder, baking soda, and salt in the bowl of a food processor and pulse to combine, 4 to 6 times. Add the butter and coconut and pulse just until the mixture resembles coarse meal, 15 to 25 times. Whisk together the egg and cream in a bowl; reserve 2 tablespoons. Add the remaining egg mixture to the butter mixture and pulse just until the mixture begins to pull away from the sides of the bowl, 20 to 30 times.

2. Turn the dough out onto a lightly floured surface and knead gently to bring the dough together, 4 to 6 times. Pat the dough to ¼ inch thickness and cut out cookies with a 2½-inch cookie cutter. Brush the cookies with the reserved egg mixture and sprinkle with raw sugar. Place the cookies, 1 inch apart, on prepared baking sheets. Bake, rotating the sheets halfway through, until golden brown, 7 to 9 minutes. Cool the baking sheets on wire racks. Repeat with the remaining cookies.

3. Spread jam on the bottom side of half of the cookies. Top with the remaining cookies.

WHITE CHOCOLATE & PEPPERMINT
BLONDIES

MAKES *18 blondies*
WORKING TIME *25 minutes*
TOTAL TIME *3 hours*

- ¾ cup (1½ sticks) unsalted butter, melted, plus more for the pan
- ¾ cup sugar
- ⅔ cup packed light brown sugar
- 3 large eggs, at room temperature
- 2 teaspoons pure vanilla extract, divided
- ¼ teaspoon pure peppermint extract
- 2⅔ cups all-purpose flour, spooned and leveled
- ¾ teaspoon baking powder
- ¼ teaspoon kosher salt
- 1½ cups coarsely chopped white chocolate
- 16 ounces cream cheese
- 1 cup confectioners' sugar
- ¾ cup peppermint candies, crushed

1. Preheat the oven to 325°F. Butter a 13×9-inch baking pan and line with parchment paper, leaving a 2-inch overhang on the long sides.

2. Whisk together the butter, sugar, brown sugar, eggs, 1 teaspoon of the vanilla, and the peppermint extract in a bowl until combined. Whisk together the flour, baking powder, and salt in a separate bowl. Stir the flour mixture into butter mixture just until combined. Stir in the chocolate. Spread the batter in a prepared pan.

3. Bake until golden brown and a toothpick inserted in the center comes out clean, 30 to 35 minutes. Cool completely in pan on a wire rack.

4. Beat the cream cheese and confectioners' sugar on medium speed with an electric mixer until light and fluffy, 1 to 2 minutes. Beat in the remaining 1 teaspoon of vanilla. Spread the frosting on the blondies; sprinkle with peppermints. Freeze until the frosting is set, 30 minutes. Lift the blondies from pan using parchment overhangs. Cut into 18 squares.

GIFT-READY PRESENTATION
Line a kraft paper box with striped wax tissue paper. Add blondies, close the box, wrap the exterior with decorative paper and red ribbon, and add a candy cane accent.

GIFT-READY PRESENTATION
Fill a six-egg carton with mini cupcake liners; add cookies. Tie the whole thing up with a bright red tag adorned with a tiny bottle brush wreath.

RED VELVET
SNOWBALLS

MAKES *about 2 dozen cookies*
WORKING TIME *20 minutes*

TOTAL TIME *1 hour, 40 minutes*

- 2½ **cups all-purpose flour, spooned and leveled**
- ¼ **cup cocoa powder**
- 2 **teaspoons baking powder**
- ¼ **teaspoon kosher salt**
- ¾ **cup unsalted butter (1½ sticks), at room temperature**

- 3 **cups confectioners' sugar, divided**
- 1 **tablespoon red food coloring**
- 1 **teaspoon pure vanilla extract**
- 1 **teaspoon white vinegar**

1. Preheat the oven to 350°F with the racks in the upper and lower thirds. Line two baking sheets with parchment paper. Whisk together the flour, cocoa, baking powder, and salt in a bowl.

2. Beat the butter and 1½ cups of the confectioners' sugar on medium speed with an electric mixer until smooth, 1 to 2 minutes. Reduce the mixer speed to low and gradually add the flour mixture, beating just until incorporated, 1 to 2 minutes. Add the food coloring, vanilla, and vinegar; increase the mixer speed to medium, and beat just until dough forms large crumbs, 15 to 20 seconds.

3. Shape the dough into balls (about 2 tablespoons each). Place the balls, 1 inch apart, on prepared baking sheets; freeze 10 minutes. Bake, rotating the sheets halfway through, until dry around the edges, 15 to 18 minutes. Cool on baking sheets on wire racks 5 minutes.

4. Place the remaining 1½ cups confectioners' sugar in a bowl. Working one at a time, gently toss the warm cookies in the sugar to coat. Return the cookies to baking sheets to cool completely; reserve the remaining sugar. Once cool, toss again, in batches, in the remaining sugar.

These melt-in-your-mouth shortbread cookies can be made up to three days in advance. Just store them in an airtight container at room temperature.

SNOWY BUTTER
BUTTONS

MAKES *32 cookies*
WORKING TIME *25 minutes*
TOTAL TIME *2 hours*

2¼ cups all-purpose flour, spooned and leveled

¾ teaspoon fine salt

1 cup (2 sticks) unsalted butter, at room temperature

2 cups confectioners' sugar, divided

1 teaspoon pure vanilla extract

1. Preheat the oven to 350°F. Whisk together the flour and salt in a bowl. Beat the butter on medium speed with an electric mixer until creamy, 2 to 3 minutes. Gradually beat in ¾ cup of the sugar, until light and fluffy, 1 to 2 minutes. Beat in the vanilla. Gradually add the flour mixture, beating just until a dough comes together.

2. Shape dough into 32 (1¼-inch round) balls (about 1 tablespoon each). Chill, covered, at least 1 hour or overnight.

3. Place the balls, 1 inch apart, on a baking sheet. Bake, rotating the baking sheet once, until golden on the bottom, 18 to 20 minutes.

4. Working one at a time, gently roll the warm cookies in the remaining 1¼ cups sugar; reserve the remaining sugar. Transfer the cookies to a wire rack to cool completely. Sprinkle the cookies with the reserved sugar.

GIFT-READY PRESENTATION
Try a sweet new twist on a souvenir snow globe and fill the bottom of an airtight jar with snowball cookies and small plastic trinkets. Use a fine-tipped brush to paint white dots on the outside of the jar, and tie a gift tag to the jar with ribbon.

Why not . . .
Revive the Lost Art of Caroling?

Imagine: You're sitting on your couch, watching a doom-and-gloom news broadcast, when—wait, what's that?—you hear strangers who have huddled in the cold to simply stand outside your door and . . . sing. And just like that, your faith in humanity is restored. Spread cheer this year by downloading free sheet music from the web, assembling a group of friends, bundling up, and hitting the streets. No iPhones allowed.

GIFT-READY PRESENTATION
Place cookies in a glassine bag, hole-punch the top of the bag and a decorative card, then secure with a pretty ribbon.

SHORTCUT SUGAR
COOKIES

MAKES *about 4 dozen cookies*
WORKING TIME *35 minutes*
TOTAL TIME *1 hour, 20 minutes*

1 (16.5 ounce) package refrigerated ready-made sugar cookie dough

½ cup all-purpose flour, spooned and leveled, plus more for surface and pressing cookies

Glass with a 2-inch decorative fluted bottom

Decorative sugars and candies

1. On a well-floured surface, knead the dough until soft. Knead the flour into dough until incorporated.

2. On a floured surface, roll the dough ⅜ inch thick. Cut cookies using a 2-inch round cutter. Dip the bottom of the glass in flour and firmly press the cookies to create a pattern. Sprinkle with sanding sugar. Reroll the dough as necessary.

3. Bake according to package directions. Press candy into warm cookies. Cool completely on a wire rack.

CANDIED
POPCORN STARS

MAKES *8 stars*
WORKING TIME *10 minutes*
TOTAL TIME *30 minutes*

1 cup sugar
⅓ cup light corn syrup
2 tablespoons butter
¼ teaspoon salt
1 teaspoon vanilla
8 cups popped corn
⅓ cup red and/or green nonpareils
¼ cup cinnamon candies

1. Combine the sugar, corn syrup, and butter with ⅓ cup of water in a heavy saucepan. Cook over medium-low heat, stirring often, until the butter melts and the sugar dissolves. Increase the heat to medium; bring to a boil. Cook, without stirring, until a candy thermometer registers 255°F.

2. Remove from the heat; stir in the salt and vanilla. Quickly pour the mixture over the popcorn; toss gently to coat. Add the nonpareils and cinnamon candies, tossing gently to combine.

3. Moisten or grease your hands. Working quickly, press the mixture into a greased 5-inch star-shaped cookie cutter, a handful at a time. If the candied corn becomes too hard to shape, place in a warm (200°F) oven for a few minutes to soften.

GIFT-READY PRESENTATION
Stack four cookies in a clear plastic bag, then tie decorative ribbon at each end of the bag to cinch. Trim ends and add a metal-rim tag.

TRIPLE-CHOCOLATE HAZELNUT
COOKIES

MAKES *about 4 dozen cookies*
WORKING TIME *20 minutes*
TOTAL TIME *1 hour, 45 minutes*

3½ cups all-purpose flour, spooned and leveled

1 cup sugar

1 cup packed light brown sugar

2 teaspoons baking powder

1 teaspoon kosher salt

½ teaspoon baking soda

½ teaspoon instant coffee powder

1 cup cocoa powder

¾ cup canola oil

¾ cup chocolate-hazelnut spread

2 large eggs, at room temperature

1 teaspoon pure vanilla extract

1½ cups coarsely chopped bittersweet chocolate

1 cup coarsely chopped toasted hazelnuts

2 teaspoons flaked sea salt

1. Preheat the oven to 350°F with the racks in the upper and lower thirds. Line two baking sheets with parchment paper. Whisk together the flour, sugar, brown sugar, baking powder, salt, baking soda, and coffee powder in a bowl.

2. Beat the cocoa, oil, hazelnut spread, and ¾ cup warm water on low speed with an electric mixer until combined, about 30 seconds. Add the eggs, one at a time, beating until incorporated after each addition. Beat in the vanilla. Stir the flour mixture into the cocoa mixture just until incorporated. Stir in the chocolate and hazelnuts.

3. Scoop cookies (about 2 tablespoons each), 3 inches apart, on prepared baking sheets. Sprinkle the cookies with sea salt. Bake, rotating the sheets halfway through, until dry around the edges, 12 to 14 minutes. Cool the baking sheets on wire racks for 10 minutes, then remove cookies to the racks to cool completely. Repeat with the remaining dough.

CHOCOLATE & CRANBERRY
FUDGE

MAKES *about 2 pounds*
WORKING TIME *35 minutes,*
plus infusing
TOTAL TIME *35 minutes,*
plus infusing

2 tablespoons orange liqueur
1 cup dried cranberries
   Butter or oil, for greasing
3½ cups raw sugar
14 ounces condensed milk
1 stick salted butter
2 tablespoons cocoa powder, sifted
1 teaspoon vanilla extract

1. Put the liqueur and cranberries into a small bowl, cover, and leave to infuse overnight.

2. Butter a nonstick pan measuring about 7 inches square.

3. Put the sugar in a deep (at least 6 inches, as the mixture will bubble up considerably), heavy saucepan with ¾ cup water, the condensed milk, butter, and cocoa powder. Heat slowly until the sugar has dissolved completely. Wash any sugar crystals down the side of the pan with a pastry brush dipped in water. Raise the heat and boil the syrup to the soft ball state (240°F on a sugar thermometer). To test, drop a teaspoon of the mixture into a small bowl of cold water. Bring it together with your fingers and it should form a soft ball. Immediately take the pan off the heat and dip the base into cold water to stop the temperature of the syrup rising further.

4. Let the syrup rest in the pan for 1 to 2 minutes, then, using a wooden spoon, stir in the vanilla extract and cranberries. Continue stirring until the syrup starts to grain and stiffen. Before it thickens too much, pour it into the prepared pan.

5. While it's still warm, mark out the fudge into squares and, when cool, cut into pieces. Wrap in cellophane or waxed paper.

GIFT-READY PRESENTATION
Create an edible ornament by filling cellophane cones (lined with cheerful printed or stamped paper) with individually wrapped pieces of this creamy fudge.

chocolate & cranberry fudge

chocolate & cranberry fudge

GIFT-READY PRESENTATION
Nestle the truffles in paper petit four cases and arrange them in an attractive vintage box or tin.

SLOE GIN
TRUFFLES

MAKES *about 2 dozen truffles*
WORKING TIME *about 20 minutes*
TOTAL TIME *about 30 minutes*

- 1 (3.4-ounce) container double cream
- 8 ounces dark chocolate, broken into pieces
- 2 tablespoons sloe gin
- 1 teaspoon vanilla extract
- Cocoa powder, for dusting

1. Pour the cream into a small pan and bring to a boil.

2. Put the chocolate in a heatproof bowl set over a pan of barely simmering water. Leave to melt, stirring once or twice until smooth.

3. Pour the cream into the melted chocolate, stirring until smooth. Allow the mixture to cool to room temperature before adding the sloe gin and vanilla. Beat (using beaters, not a whisk) until the mixture lightens in color and looks fluffier. Chill for 10 minutes or so to firm before forming the truffles.

4. Sift a thick layer of cocoa powder onto a tray lined with baking parchment and cover another tray with petit-four cases. Using two teaspoons, drop small, evenly sized blobs of the chocolate mixture into the cocoa. Dust your fingers with cocoa powder and quickly roll each one into a ball, then roll it in more cocoa and place inside the cases.

FRUITCAKE
COOKIES

MAKES *about 5 dozen cookies*
WORKING TIME *25 minutes*
TOTAL TIME *2 hours, 20 minutes*

1¾ cups cake flour, spooned and leveled, divided

1 teaspoon baking powder

½ teaspoon baking soda

¼ teaspoon kosher salt

⅛ teaspoon ground cinnamon

Pinch ground nutmeg

½ cup chopped toasted pecans

½ cup chopped pistachios

½ cup (1 stick) unsalted butter, at room temperature

1 cup packed dark brown sugar

1 large egg, at room temperature

1½ teaspoons pure vanilla extract, divided

1 cup finely chopped maraschino cherries, well drained

¼ cup finely chopped candied pineapple

½ cup confectioners' sugar

½ tablespoon brandy

1 to 2 teaspoons milk

1. Preheat the oven to 350°F with the racks in the upper and lower thirds. Line two baking sheets with parchment paper. Whisk 1¼ cups of the flour together with the baking powder, baking soda, salt, cinnamon, and nutmeg in a bowl. Toss the pecans and pistachios with the remaining ½ cup of flour in a separate bowl.

2. Beat the butter and brown sugar on medium speed with an electric mixer until light and fluffy, 1 to 2 minutes. Add the egg, beating until incorporated. Beat in 1 teaspoon of the vanilla. Reduce the mixer speed to low and gradually add the flour mixture, beating just until incorporated, 1 to 2 minutes. Stir in the nuts (and any flour remaining in the bowl), cherries, and pineapple until evenly incorporated. Scoop the dough (about ½ tablespoon each), 2 inches apart, on prepared baking sheets. Bake, rotating the sheets halfway through, until golden brown around the edges, 14 to 16 minutes. Cool on baking sheets on wire racks for 10 minutes; remove to the racks to cool completely.

3. Whisk together the confectioners' sugar, brandy, remaining ½ teaspoon vanilla, and 1 teaspoon milk (add an additional teaspoon of milk if the glaze is too thick). Drizzle over the cooled cookies. Let sit, at room temperature, until the glaze is set, about 30 minutes.

GIFT-READY PRESENTATION

Line a mini loaf pan with tissue paper, then wax paper. Add the cookies, fold the paper over, then wrap with a ribbon and attach a card with a miniature clothespin.

TO FROM

the *Merriest Christmas*

FOR *Will*

FROM *Sarah*

GIFT-READY PRESENTATION
Wrap the edges of a cardboard pie slice box with decorative ribbon. Wrap cookies in parchment, then secure with ribbon and tuck them inside the box.

SPICED
SHORTBREAD

MAKES *16 cookies*
WORKING TIME *15 minutes*
TOTAL TIME *1 hour, 50 minutes*

½ cup (1 stick) cold unsalted butter, cut up, plus more for pan

1½ cups whole-wheat flour, spooned and leveled

½ cup packed dark brown sugar

¼ teaspoon kosher salt

¾ teaspoon ground ginger

¼ teaspoon ground cinnamon

1. Butter a 9-inch cake pan, line the bottom with parchment paper, and butter the parchment. Place the flour, sugar, salt, ginger, and cinnamon in the bowl of a food processor and pulse to combine, 3 to 5 times. Add the butter and pulse until the mixture looks like wet sand, 40 to 50 times.

2. Press the mixture evenly into the prepared pan. Leaving a 1-inch border, prick the dough with the tines of a fork; freeze 30 minutes.

3. Preheat the oven to 350°F. Bake until set and just beginning to brown around the edges, 30 to 35 minutes.

4. Place the pan on a wire rack and immediately use the handle of a wooden spoon to press a scallop pattern into the edge of the shortbread and a sharp knife to score it into 16 wedges. Cool 10 minutes. Run a knife around the edges of the shortbread to loosen; invert onto a wire rack to cool completely. Cut along the scored lines using a sharp knife.

CHRISTMAS CANDY
CUPCAKES

MAKES *16 cupcakes*
WORKING TIME *1 hour*
TOTAL TIME *2 hours, 15 minutes*

- 2¼ cups sifted all-purpose flour (sift then measure)
- 2½ teaspoons baking powder
- ½ teaspoon kosher salt
- ¾ cup (1½ sticks) unsalted butter, at room temperature
- 1¾ cups sugar
- 2 large eggs
- 1 tablespoon pure vanilla extract
- 1 cup milk
- ½ recipe White Vanilla Frosting (see page 141)

1. Preheat the oven to 350°F. Line two standard-sized muffin tins with 16 cupcake liners. Whisk together the flour, baking powder, and salt in a bowl.

2. Beat the butter and sugar with an electric mixer on medium speed until light and fluffy, 1 to 2 minutes. Add the eggs, one at a time, beating to incorporate after each addition; add the vanilla and beat to combine. Reduce the mixer speed to low and beat in the flour mixture and milk alternately, starting and ending with the flour mixture, just until incorporated.

3. Transfer the batter to the prepared pans, dividing evenly. Bake until a toothpick inserted in the center comes out clean, 18 to 20 minutes. Cool in the pans on a wire rack for 5 minutes, then remove to rack to cool completely.

4. Frost the cupcakes and decorate:

To make holly berry cupcakes, unroll and cut green candy like Airheads® or Laffy Taffy® with a 1¾×1-inch holly leaf cookie cutter. Use a butter knife to make veins in leaves, then arrange leaves on cupcakes and use red coated chocolates like M&M's for berries.

To make Christmas wreath cupcakes, arrange mint M&M's in a circle on top of the cupcake. Use red candy balls and silver dragées to make berry clusters, and shape a small piece of red string licorice into a bow for the wreath, pinching the center to help it hold.

To make poinsettia cupcakes, cut large marshmallows crosswise into five pieces. Sprinkle one cut edge with red sanding sugar. Overlap marshmallow pieces on cupcakes to form a flower and attach mini yellow M&M's with a dab of frosting for the center.

The candy decorations lend these Christmas cupcakes an extra-festive touch.

PINECONE BROWNIE
WREATH

MAKES *10 servings*
WORKING TIME *50 minutes*
TOTAL TIME *2 hours*

Cooking spray

1¼ cups all-purpose flour, spooned and leveled

1 teaspoon ground cinnamon

1 cup (2 sticks) unsalted butter

8 ounces bittersweet chocolate chips

4 large eggs, at room temperature

1½ cups sugar

½ cup packed dark brown sugar

2 teaspoons pure vanilla extract

½ teaspoon kosher salt

Tootsie Roll® candies

1. Preheat the oven to 350°F. Spray a 9×13-inch baking pan with cooking spray and line with parchment paper, leaving a 2-inch overhang on the long sides. Whisk together the flour and cinnamon in a bowl.

2. Melt the butter and chocolate together in a microwave, stirring at 20-second intervals, until melted and thoroughly combined, 1 to 2 minutes.

3. Whisk the eggs in a separate bowl. Add the sugar, brown sugar, vanilla, and salt and whisk until combined. Whisk in the chocolate mixture and then the flour mixture until just combined. Pour the batter into prepared pan.

4. Bake until a toothpick inserted in the center comes out clean, 30 to 32 minutes. Cool in the pan on a wire rack. Run a paring knife around the edge of pan to loosen the brownies. Use the parchment to lift the brownies from the pan.

5. Use various-sized round cookie cutters to cut brownies.

6. Use scissors to snip Tootsie Roll® candies crosswise into ½-inch pieces. Layer and build them up on several of the brownies to create pinecone petals.

7. Arrange the brownies in a circle, stacking a few to create height. Decorate with a ribbon bow, if desired.

Christmas Collectibles

Iconic Bakeware

Pie filling–stained recipe cards aside, what could provide better baking inspiration than time-tested tools passed down from a family member (or painstakingly collected at years of yard sales and flea markets)? Whether they're part of your treat-making tool kit or just eye candy, here's a look at vintage bakeware that really takes the cake.

Oak is a German symbol for strength, making the acorn a common springerle motif.

Springerle cookie molds

These intricate templates originated in Germany in the 14th century. ("Springerle" is German for "little knight.") Many U.S. models are from the 1800s, when the country saw an influx of German immigrants. Expect to see plenty of traditional German icons, including edelweiss flowers, acorns, or scenes celebrating the harvest, and to pay according to the mold's age and condition.

Rolling pins

Turned-wood versions of these baking tools have been around since at least the 1600s (and likely longer), and the styles that have spun off since then are almost too numerous to count: the hollow glass versions from the mid-19th century that sailors filled with cocoa and baking powder for their beloveds back home; the porcelain Delft models, with their pretty blue patterns; and heavy stoneware pins, which are among the rarest antique styles to unearth today. While some certainly fetch higher prices than others, collecting these beautifully utilitarian tools is all ultimately a matter of personal taste.

Cast-iron pans

In the 1850s, American foundries moved beyond the famed skillet and debuted specialty pans that are still hot today. Griswold, the maker of the heart and stars pan, is considered the most desirable American maker because of the quality of iron. A Griswold lidded loaf pan (used for both meatloaf and bread) in pristine condition might go for an impressive $1,600 today.

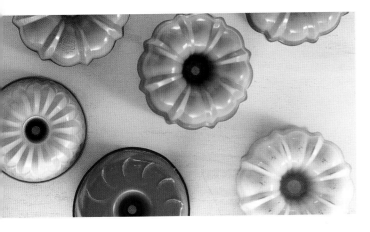

Tube pans

In 1950, Nordic Ware introduced the Bundt® pan and the term has since become synonymous with ring-shaped pans. The original Bundt pan had a plain metal finish, and sales were so poor, the company considered discontinuing. Instead, they introduced colors—the blue shown here is a rare and desirable hue. When the Bundt pan became a hit, many companies copied the design, often using cheaper materials. Instead of heavy cast aluminum, they were often made of thinner stamped aluminum, as is the case with the cheery orange version.

In England, "pudding" is a general term for desserts of all kinds, hence the term "pudding mold."

Copper pudding molds

Gleaming and ornate, these fanciful casts originated in Europe in the 1700s and remained au courant through World War I. While even unmarked versions pack a visual punch, unusual forms from esteemed makers such as Trottier (of France) and Benham & Froud (of England) can be worth several hundred dollars apiece.

countdown

THE 12 DAYS OF DECORATING

- - - - - - - - -

Keep the drummers, dancers, and milkmaids. Here's to ringing in the season with 12 days of doable DIYs. We're talking about handmade ornament upgrades, fresh ideas for displaying greenery, all-new twists on advent calendars, and colorful, one-of-a-kind wreaths.

Humble coffee filters gathered into lush blooms can become a pretty and perky garland for a holiday mantel.

12 Easy Ornaments

| № 2 |

Baking Molds

Vintage baking molds add a sweet touch to any tree; simply **hot-glue ribbon** loops to their backs and hang.

| № 1 |

Upgrade a Plain Glass Ornament

At around a dollar each, these empty **orbs** offer an affordable catalyst for creativity. Fill one with **small wooden chips**, another with a single **stunning peacock feather** (attached to the ornament's top with **hot glue**). Or compose a more obvious Christmas scene by dropping **a model fir tree** into a globe dusted with **artificial snow**. You can also use **tweezers** to position **branches** inside and even hot-glue a **tiny cardinal** in place.

Cheerful chirpers

Paint cardboard, then **cut** in the shape of a goose, dove, or robin, and equip with a **loop** at the top for hanging. For an ornament that does double duty as decor for the front of a handmade holiday card, make a horizontal cut in the top of **a blank card**, about ½ inch from the top edge, push the **ribbon** through the slot in the card, tie into a knot, and allow the bird to hang freely on the front.

No 4

Sparkling Ornaments

We turned old **night-light bulbs** into festive ornaments, but any size will do. Just brush on **glittering glue**, roll the bulb in glitter, and let dry for 15 minutes. Then **hot-glue** a loop of **metallic embroidery floss** to the bulb's base.

| № 5 |

Patchwork balls

Cover a **Styrofoam ball** with **scraps of coordinating fabric**, using the dull edge of a **knife** to press in the edges. Continue until everything is tucked in, then **sew** on a loop of **twine** to hang. ▶

| № 6 |

Salvaged sweater hoop

Fit the inner circle of a **3-inch embroidery hoop** over the desired section of **an old scarf or sweater**. Cut out the section, leaving a ½-inch edge. Fold excess fabric over hoop and **hot-glue** in back. Attach outer hoop and thread **ribbon** through hardware at top to hang.

| № 7 | Ribbon candy ornaments

Fold a length of **ribbon**—a striped design works well—into loops as shown and pass a **needle** threaded with **strong cotton thread** through its center, adding a **stack of buttons** at either end. Tie a knot at both ends to secure, then create a loop of thread for hanging.

BRIGHT IDEA
Paint these with a classic Scandi pattern yourself, or turn it into a fun creative project for children.

TO MAKE
clay dala horses

1. Start with a pack of white oven-bake clay, an old rolling pin (no longer used for food), and a Dala horse-shaped cookie cutter. Roll out one sheet of clay evenly to $3/16$ inch thick (any less and the decorations will be too fragile and break).

2. Cut out several horses using the cookie cutter. Press the excess clay together and roll it out again to make more horses. Repeat with another piece if needed.

3. Determine where the hole for the ribbon should be on each horse. Prior to making a hole, hold each horse between your fingertips to simulate it hanging from a ribbon to ensure each one will hang level.

4. Using a knitting needle or wooden skewer, make a hole ¼ inch from the outer edge, moving the needle in a circular motion to make it big enough.

5. Follow the package instructions for baking the clay in the oven.

6. When the decorations have hardened, tidy up any rough edges with a craft knife.

7. Using watered-down red acrylic paint, paint your designs; when dry, do the same on the reverse.

8. Once the paint on all the decorations has dried, thread a length of twine through each to hang.

| Nº 9 |

Pretty paper shields

Glue **a sheet of wrapping paper** to either side of a **lightweight** piece of **cardstock** using **spray mount**. Create a shield-shaped template from another piece of **cardstock or cardboard**, and place it on the paper-covered card. Trace the template, then cut out the shape. Make a hole in the top with a **hole punch** and use a length of **fine rickrack** to create a loop for hanging.

BRIGHT IDEA
Hang these lighter, brighter fall standbys from your chandelier with colorful velvet ribbon.

| Nº 10 |

TO MAKE
frosted pinecones

1. Mix two parts bleach with one part water in a bucket. Submerge pinecones in the solution for 24 hours. (**TIP** Place a plate or another heavy object on top to keep them under water.) Rinse them in water and set them outside to dry until they open up again. (This could take up to a week, depending on the weather.)

2. Cut 1 yard of velvet ribbon into a ¾-yard piece and a ¼-yard piece.

3. Adhere the end of the longer ribbon to the pinecone base with hot glue. Tie the shorter ribbon into a bow, and adhere to the base of the pinecone, as shown.

| № 11 |

Fabric evergreen

Cut out **two equal-size fabric triangles** with **pinking shears** and place the wrong sides together. **Sew** into a tree shape on the two long edges using a fine running stitch. Fill the triangle with **cotton stuffing** and sew closed. Sew a loop of **twine** to the top.

BRIGHT IDEA
Thread these lemon and vanilla cookies onto string and hang on the tree or from twiggy arrangements.

| Nº 12 | SWEET HEARTS
COOKIE ORNAMENTS

MAKES *14 cookies*
WORKING TIME *30 minutes,*
plus chilling
TOTAL TIME *42 minutes,*
plus chilling

1 stick butter, softened
   Zest of 1 lemon
¼ cup fine sugar
1 medium egg yolk
1 teaspoon vanilla extract
1 cup plain flour
¼ cup cornflour
2 ounces ground almonds

1. Beat together the butter, zest, sugar, egg yolk, and vanilla until fluffy and lighter in color.

2. Sift together the flour, cornflour, and almonds, then blend into the butter mixture to make a dough. Turn out onto a lightly floured work surface and knead until smooth. Flatten into a disc, wrap in plastic wrap, and chill until firm enough to roll.

3. Roll out the dough between two sheets of parchment paper to ³⁄₁₆ inch thick. Stamp out 14 heart shapes using a 3-inch cutter, rerolling the trimmings if necessary. Using a skewer, make small holes near the tops of the hearts for threading onto string later. Transfer to two baking sheets and chill for 20 minutes until firm.

4. Preheat the oven to 350°F. Bake the cookies for 10 to 12 minutes, until lightly golden at the edges. Leave the cookies on the baking sheets for 3 to 4 minutes to firm up before transferring to wire racks to cool. If the holes have closed up slightly during cooking, make them larger again while the cookies are still hot.

11 Natural Elements

| № 1 | **Leafy chandelier**

To create a hanging Scandinavian-style candle garland above the table, start with **a willow base** and weave greenery around it, including **ivy, myrtle, and scented eucalyptus**. Use **robust clip holders** (with wide surrounds for catching hot wax drips) to fix half a dozen candles securely in place, then attach **strong cords** (wound with more foliage) to hang the wreath from a ceiling hook.

| № 2 | **Woodland candleholders**

Cut a piece of **silver birch bark**—you can buy it in sheets—to the desired size with a strong pair of **florist's scissors or a craft knife**. Roll into a cylinder and secure with **florist's wire** and **natural ribbon** tied in a double knot. Fill with **moss**. Wrap the bottom of a **taper candle** with **foil** (to prevent the moss from burning), and place the taper in the center of the moss. If you have a few **beads, thread** one onto **a sprig of spruce**, then tuck the foliage under the ribbon to finish.

| № 3 |

Fruit stand

Filling **bowls, baskets, and platters** with **crisp red or green apples** is one of the simplest seasonal styling tricks around.

| № 4 |

A new twist on willow

Add instant holiday cheer to a hallway table with this simple rustic heart. Just bend a few lengths of **fresh-cut green willow** into two adjacent arcs and secure with florist's wire or twine at the base and apex. Trim the ends and decorate with **sprigs of mistletoe** and a **brightly colored ribbon**.

Welcome wreath

Dish out some hospitality with this charming alternative to a typical wreath. Simply apply a layer of **chalkboard paint** to the inside of an old tray, then add seasonal **branches** or **evergreen and holly** for a festive finish.

Welcome to our Home

№ 6 | **Flurry vision**

Fill the bottom of an **old jam jar** with **salt** (to look like snow) and place a **tealight** or **short candle** inside. Tie a length of **string** around the top to make a handle.

| № 7 |

Cloche encounters

Pile **pinecones, paperwhites, or pomegranates** under a glass **cloche** for an easy (and affordable) display.

| № 8 |

Branch dressing

Hang up a **twiggy branch**, then decorate it with **colorful ornaments and ribbons** to twinkle like a chandelier. Interestingly shaped cuttings, like this lichen-covered one, will give the best effect.

TO MAKE
straw wreaths

1. To make a charming accent for dining room chairs, cut a 24-inch length of wire and bend it into a horseshoe shape. (We used armature wire, but any wire, including a coat hanger, will work.) Wrap the wire, including any sharp ends, with masking tape.

2. Gather five pieces of dried wheat and trim the stems to 2½ inches long. Wrap the stems together with white, cloth-covered floral wire to make a bundle. Make nine more bundles of five stems each, for a total of 10 bundles.

3. Attach the bundles to the horseshoe-shaped wire with floral wire. Place five on the right and five on the left, leaving a 2-inch space at the center. Tie a bow with 1 yard of ribbon in this space.

4. Use additional floral wire to secure the arms and center to the back of a chair. Repeat for each chair in your set.

| № 10 |

A slice of life

There's something sad about parting ways with a Christmas tree at the end of each season. Battle the post-holiday blues by creating a sentimental (and sappy!) reminder of Christmases past. Simply **saw** off a thin, dry slice of **your tree's trunk** and use a **wood-burning pen** to document the year and, if you choose, a special holiday memory. ("Charlie got a new bike!" or "Sara got engaged!")

| No 11 | **Sheaf tricks**

Bundle **a small handful of wheat** and tie with **brightly colored twine**. Turn a **cloche** upside down and place the wheat inside, then top with the base and invert. If you like, you can add leftover snips of wheat to **votive holders** and secure with the same twine.

10 Ways to Display Cards

| № 1 | In a tobacco basket

Show off the influx of season's greetings on a **vintage tobacco basket** by tucking cards and photos into the overlapping strips of reed.

| № 2 |

In tree-shaped tiers

1. **Cut a piece of bamboo or dowel** into five different lengths, so that they measure 8 inches, 10 inches, 12 inches, 14 inches, and 16 inches long.

2. **Cut** a length of **sturdy, wide patterned ribbon** to reach from the top of the door down to the door handle.

3. Arrange the rods along the ribbon at equal intervals with the longest piece at the bottom and the shortest piece at the top, and attach to the back of the ribbon using **a glue gun**.

4. Display the cards along the rods with **colorful clothespins or binder clips**.

| № 3 | On a wooden ladder

An old orchard staple becomes a fruitful display for colorful cards, secured with **clothespins** and string along one side.

| № 4 |

Bring the outdoors in

Twine, clothespins, and nature-themed cards pair up for a charming, low-key display.

| № 5 | ## On ruler stars—small, medium, and large—that all measure up

To make a small ruler star, gather **five 12-inch rulers**. Place them in a star shape, as shown. Secure each end with **hot glue**. To make a medium ruler star, bend a **5-foot folding ruler** at every segment to form a six-pointed star. Hot-glue the ends together to secure. To make a large ruler star, bend **two 6-foot folding rulers** at every foot. Overlap the first and last sections, forming a star shape as shown. Secure the overlapped sections with **binder clips**. Use more binder clips or **clothespins** to attach cards to each star.

An antique coaster can become a backdrop for an avalanche of Christmas greetings.

| № 6 | **Along a ribbon**

Decorative, **brightly colored clips**—or even regular old **binder clips in red and green**—are a no-fuss (yet still festive) way to display cards. These dangle sweetly from **a length of ribbon** strung from an iron bed frame.

| No. 8 | **Alongside ornaments**

Intersperse with **ornaments** along a zigzagged length of **twine** for more visual appeal.

| No. 9 | **In a picture frame**

Holiday greeting cards take on the appearance of art when strung up inside an empty **picture frame** with embellishments such as **holly** and **tree sprigs**.

[A368]

10

Christmas Tree Display

Overflowing with good tidings, this **tree** displays holiday greeting cards clipped to **jute twine** with **mini clothespins**.

| No 2 |

Goody bags

Sew **24 drawstring bags** from a collection of fabrics in similar colors. For the numbers, use a **stencil** and **fabric paint** to mark a small piece of vintage linen, and **sew** the cloth onto the bag. Fill each one with **a sweet treat or small toy**. Run a length of ribbon through a hem at the top of every bag and tie them onto a length of **string**.

| No 3 |

Sweet somethings

Ceramic cups filled with **candies** and adorned with hand-**painted** numerals make for a fun twist on the typical countdown.

| № 4 |

Pot luck

Tiny **planters** suspended from
wire and string can also make
delightful places to bury **small
gifts** and surprises.

| No 5 |

Bucket list

Attach **tiny metal pails** to sturdy **red-and-white-striped ribbon** and number them with **permanent marker or paint**.

| No 6 |

MAKE
a better bunting

1. Draw a triangle the size you would like your bunting flags to be onto a piece of paper. (The triangles should have two sides of equal length and one short side.)

2. Cut out the triangle and trace the outline onto a piece of cardboard. Flip the triangle along one long edge and trace around it, then flip it along the other long edge and trace again so you have three wedge shapes fanning out beside each other. Now draw a triangle "hat" on the short side of the middle triangle (this will be the flap that closes each pocket). This is your template for all your flags.

3. Trace around the template onto your chosen wrapping papers (scraps work perfectly), cut out, and fold along the long edges of the middle triangle so it resembles a flattened cone. Repeat 23 times to create enough flags for an advent calendar.

4. Use double-sided tape to fix the long sides into place.

5. Stamp or write the numbers 1 through 24 on stickers.

6. Fill each pocket with treats, fold down the flap, and stick into place with a sticker. Attach the flags to a ribbon with clothespins or paperclips.

| № 7 |

Toys and trinkets

Hung inside an **old hotel key cabinet**, numbered **gift tags** adorned with tiny **ornaments** build anticipation with antiques.

| № 8 |

The name game

Let each guest play Santa for a day. Instead of candy, fill advent calendar **pouches** (like the stamped muslin ones shown here) with guests' names, then let that day's Saint Nick choose the activity, from caroling to cookie making.

BRIGHT IDEA
Collect shiny gold ornaments under a generous cloche for a sparkling and sculptural display.

7 Stocking Upgrades

| No 1 |

MAKE IT PERSONAL!
Add a name or monogram with the same technique you used for the snowflake.

NO-SEW
cross-stitch

1. Download our template from clv.h-cdn.co/assets/ cm/15/27/559438cb6d13f_-_ Stocking.pdf. Trace and cut the stocking front from 11-count Aida cloth. Use a marker to shade in the heel and toe as shown. Draw Xs with a fine-tip marker to create the snowflake.

2. For the cuff, cut a 7½-inch wide by 3-inch high piece of Aida cloth and shade in with a marker. Fold the edges and affix with fabric glue to hem.

3. Trace and cut the stocking back from red felt. Fold the edges of both stocking pieces, and line the edges with fabric glue. Affix to the back. Glue the cuff as shown.

4. Use a felt scrap to create a hanger for the stocking.

The same stocking pattern mentioned at left can be used to make each of these.

| №️ 6 |

Plaid tidings

Give tattered **plaid blankets** and **scarves** new life by transforming them into stockings with fringe. You can do the same with old quilts and Pendleton or Hudson's Bay blankets.

| №️ 2-5 |

Down-home danglers

Adapt a **grain sack** to be filled with delicious dry goods. A **gingham** style shows Santa precisely where to check in. **Ticking stripe** fabric with a candy cane-like edging bodes well for sweets. Stitch up a **seed sack** stocking and plant it on the mantel for a graphic touch.

| №️ 7 |

Swap socks for a box

Replace stockings with **vintage crates**. Give each guest a special delivery on Christmas morning by corralling gifts in tagged shipping crates under the tree.

6 Cheerful Paper Crafts

| № 1 |

Party-ready lanterns

Cut slits along the central section of a piece of **patterned paper**. Score along the middle of each line. **Glue** the ends of the paper together to make a tube shape, and scrunch to bend the paper along the scored lines.

| № 2 |

Folk art forest

Draw and cut out a large and small tree template from a **piece of cardboard**. Trace the shapes onto white cardstock several times and cut out. Fold the tree shapes in half, and use a **craft knife** to cut fine folk-art patterns on the branches and down the center of the trees. Unfold and **stick** the trunks to a strip of **thick cardstock** for stability, and display along a ledge or mantel.

| №3 |

Star track

Using **adhesive spray**, attach **patterned paper** to both sides of a piece of **lightweight cardstock**. Draw star shapes and cut out with a **craft knife**. Make six small holes with a **wooden skewer or rotary hole punch**, and, using **twine and a needle**, sew three lines to make a star effect, starting and finishing at the two holes on either side so it hangs evenly.

| № 4 |

Faux-bois garland

Using **hand-drawn templates**, cut out a mix of different leaf shapes from **plain cardstock or paper**, or try scraps of **wrapping paper** in a cheeky faux-bois design. **Punch a hole** in the top of each leaf and string the leaves along a length of **twine** to decorate a shelf or mirror. Hang **fairy lights** behind to illuminate.

| № 5 |

Wintry wreath

Cut out an array of leaf shapes from **white paper**, fold each one in half to give it definition, then attach with **double-sided tape** (working in one direction) to **a Styrofoam wreath base**.

| № 6 |

Color wheels

Cut two strips of **bright gift wrap** or **craft paper** measuring 12 inches by 2 inches. Fold them, accordion-style, then stick them together along two short edges to form one long strip. Fan the pleats out to make a complete circle, stick the two remaining edges together to secure them, and **glue** or **stitch** a **button** through the center to finish. Hang on the tree, gather in a candy dish, or scatter across a table for a whimsical effect.

5 Needle-Free Trees

BRIGHT IDEA
Use a cookie cutter wrapped in tinsel for the star on top.

|№ 1| **Tin tower**

Stack **cookie and candy containers** from largest to smallest, then wrap with a garland made of **baker's twine** and **candy**.

|№ 2| **Christmas kerchiefs**

Use pushpins to secure **green handkerchiefs** (and a brown hankie "stump") to the wall or a **bulletin board** for a nothing-to-sniff-at display.

| № 3 | All aboard

Paint a tree on a **shipping crate** and embellish the slats with **pompoms**.

| № 4 | Garden variety

Turn a **tomato cage** upside down, place it in a **galvanized bucket**, and decorate liberally with **Shiny Brites** or an assortment of tomato-red ornaments.

| № 5 | Great pyramid

Fill six like-size **canning jars** with **ornaments, tinsel, or greenery**. Stack the jars in descending numbers as shown, then wrap with a **shiny garland** and top with a **star**.

4 Collectibles-Clad Wreaths

| № 1 | **Take note**

Cut **four pages of sheet music** (preferably holiday carols) into ½-inch strips and wrap around a **12-inch Styrofoam wreath form**, attaching with **clear tape**.

| № 2 |

Have a ball

Wrap a **Styrofoam wreath form** with **ribbon** and use **greening pins** to attach different shapes and sizes of **Shiny Brites**. To cover a 16-inch form, you'll need about 100 ornaments.

| № 3 |

Wrap it up

Wrap a **16-inch Styrofoam wreath form** with **fluffy tinsel**, using **U-shaped wire greening pins** to secure ends.

| № 4 |

Light show

Hot-glue two layers of **vintage Christmas lights** (you'll need about 65 bulbs) to a flat, **12-inch craft ring**.

3 Takes On Garlands

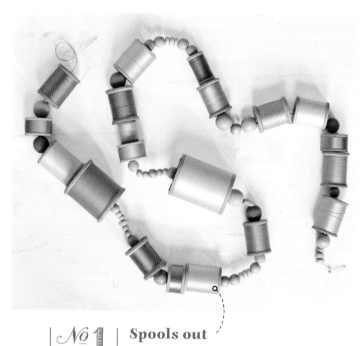

| No 1 | Spools out

Thread **spools of varying sizes and hues** (interspersed with **colorful wooden beads**) on **a long piece of embroidery thread**. Knot ends to secure.

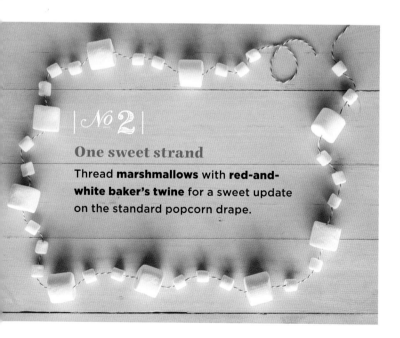

| No 2 |

One sweet strand

Thread **marshmallows** with **red-and-white baker's twine** for a sweet update on the standard popcorn drape.

TO MAKE
perky papers

1. Stack 12 ruffled coffee filters, randomly mixing white and natural-colored ones, and staple the center. Poke a hole near the center of each stack with a small nail.

2. Cut a piece of twine that's at least 1 foot longer than the desired length of your garland, and knot one end. Thread on one stack and secure tightly in place by knotting the twine on the other side, then tie another knot 6 inches down. Slide on a second stack until it presses against that last knot.

3. Continue tying knots and adding stacks until all are strung.

4. Finally, scrunch the filters with your fingers to transform each stack into a full-fledged pompom.

2 Cozy Cushions

| No 1 |

| No 2 | **Cheery pillow**

Take a **plain pillow** from ho-hum to ho-ho-ho merely by wrapping it up like a present. (Yes, it's that simple.) We used **1½-inch twill tape** to spruce this one up; add a **sprig of greenery** or a **festive ornament** for an extra bit of flourish.

TO MAKE
an upholstered pouf

One thing's a given at the holidays: You can always use more seating. This DIY option uses grain sacks (or striped fabric inspired by them) to create a relaxed part-time perch.

1. Starting with 3½ yards of grain-sack fabric, cut out nine 8½×26-inch rectangles, centering the stripes on each rectangle.

2. Sew the pieces right sides together along the long edges, creating a large rectangle. Fold the rectangle in half, right sides together, and then sew the remaining long edges together to create a tube. Turn the tube right side out. Fold a pleat 2 inches from the left-hand corner of each panel; tack down the pleat with a stitch. Repeat on other end of the panel.

3. Cut two circles of fabric 16 inches in diameter for the top and bottom of the pouf. Fold a ½-inch hem around the end of each circle. Using a running stitch, hand-sew one circle to one end of the tube, 1½ inches from the edge of the tube. Repeat with the second circle on the other end, leaving a small opening in the bottom for stuffing.

4. Stuff with beanbag filler, and hand-stitch the opening closed.

1 Christmas Fairy

. . . to hang on the tree or pose in a seasonal scene

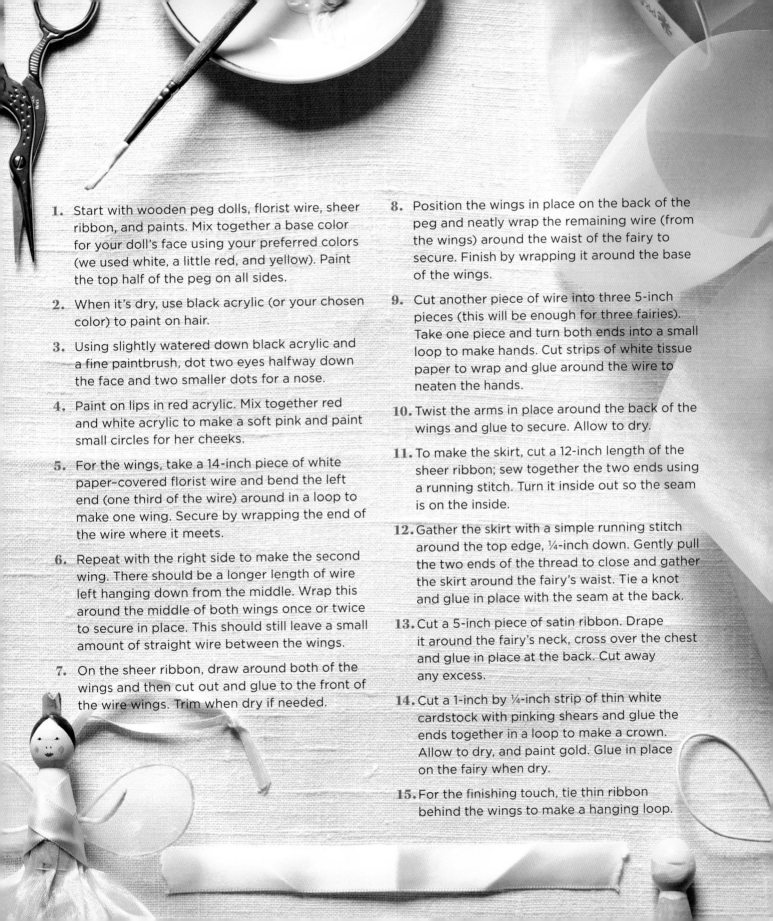

1. Start with wooden peg dolls, florist wire, sheer ribbon, and paints. Mix together a base color for your doll's face using your preferred colors (we used white, a little red, and yellow). Paint the top half of the peg on all sides.

2. When it's dry, use black acrylic (or your chosen color) to paint on hair.

3. Using slightly watered down black acrylic and a fine paintbrush, dot two eyes halfway down the face and two smaller dots for a nose.

4. Paint on lips in red acrylic. Mix together red and white acrylic to make a soft pink and paint small circles for her cheeks.

5. For the wings, take a 14-inch piece of white paper–covered florist wire and bend the left end (one third of the wire) around in a loop to make one wing. Secure by wrapping the end of the wire where it meets.

6. Repeat with the right side to make the second wing. There should be a longer length of wire left hanging down from the middle. Wrap this around the middle of both wings once or twice to secure in place. This should still leave a small amount of straight wire between the wings.

7. On the sheer ribbon, draw around both of the wings and then cut out and glue to the front of the wire wings. Trim when dry if needed.

8. Position the wings in place on the back of the peg and neatly wrap the remaining wire (from the wings) around the waist of the fairy to secure. Finish by wrapping it around the base of the wings.

9. Cut another piece of wire into three 5-inch pieces (this will be enough for three fairies). Take one piece and turn both ends into a small loop to make hands. Cut strips of white tissue paper to wrap and glue around the wire to neaten the hands.

10. Twist the arms in place around the back of the wings and glue to secure. Allow to dry.

11. To make the skirt, cut a 12-inch length of the sheer ribbon; sew together the two ends using a running stitch. Turn it inside out so the seam is on the inside.

12. Gather the skirt with a simple running stitch around the top edge, ¼-inch down. Gently pull the two ends of the thread to close and gather the skirt around the fairy's waist. Tie a knot and glue in place with the seam at the back.

13. Cut a 5-inch piece of satin ribbon. Drape it around the fairy's neck, cross over the chest and glue in place at the back. Cut away any excess.

14. Cut a 1-inch by ¼-inch strip of thin white cardstock with pinking shears and glue the ends together in a loop to make a crown. Allow to dry, and paint gold. Glue in place on the fairy when dry.

15. For the finishing touch, tie thin ribbon behind the wings to make a hanging loop.

celebrate

MEMORABLE MEALS

Whether you've cooked two Christmas dinners or two dozen, each year is a little bit different from the last. Maybe your kids have grown into new tastes (or out of old ones), or you've fallen hard for a dish your in-laws brought over last year and are determined to work into your repertoire. If you're looking to mix up your main course routine or just add some variety to the menu, here are enticing entrees, side dish upgrades, and irresistible desserts worth considering. Who knows? You might stumble onto a new specialty of your very own.

Even a well-stocked (and oft-consulted) recipe box can make room for a few new (or improved) additions. The following pages contain plenty of appetizing candidates.

nibble

CROWD-PLEASING APPETIZERS, SIDES, AND SIPS

- - - - - - - - - - - -

How about we (finally) stop calling them sides, because we all know that the army of veggies, breads, salads, and starches that fill our tables (and our plates) are just as essential as the turkey. (Not to mention the nibbles we try not to fill up on before dinner starts.) It's time to bring sides front and center, where they belong.

All the dishes pictured here call for five ingredients or fewer (not counting pantry staples like butter, oil, salt, pepper, and spices).

Turn to page 230–231 for the recipes for these holiday-menu mainstays—made easy.

Let the bread-breaking commence! These easy two-bite crostini will give guests something to graze on as you fiddle with the main course.

Twelve Twists on Crostini

1 BLUEBERRY & JALAPEÑO

Combine ⅔ **cup ricotta, 1 chopped scallion**, and **kosher salt**. Top **16 toasted baguette slices** with the ricotta mixture, **3 tablespoons blueberry jam**, and **sliced jalapeño**.

2 BEET HUMMUS & CHICKPEA

Process **15½ ounces chickpeas, 1 cooked beet, ¼ cup olive oil, 3 tablespoons mint, 2 garlic cloves, 1 tablespoon lemon juice, ¾ teaspoon ground cumin**, and **kosher salt** in a food processor until smooth. Top **16 toasted baguette slices** with beet hummus, **crunchy chickpeas**, and mint.

3 PICKLED SHALLOT & CUCUMBER

Bring **1 tablespoon red wine vinegar, 1 teaspoon sugar, 1 teaspoon kosher salt**, and 2 tablespoons water to a boil. Turn off the heat and add **1 sliced shallot** and let stand until softened, 10 to 12 minutes; drain. Top **16 toasted baguette slices** with **4 ounces Boursin° cheese, thinly sliced cucumber,** and **pickled shallots**.

4 MANGO & PEPPER JELLY

Combine ½ **chopped mango,** ⅓ **cup pepper jelly, 1 teaspoon lime zest**, and **1 teaspoon lime juice**. Top **16 toasted baguette slices** with **4 ounces goat cheese** and the mango mixture.

5 PIMIENTO CHEESE & BACON

Stir together **8 ounces grated extra-sharp Cheddar cheese, ¼ cup mayonnaise, 1 (4-ounce) jar diced pimientos** (drained), **1 teaspoon Dijon mustard**, and ⅛ **teaspoon cayenne**. Top **16 toasted baguette slices** with the pimiento cheese, **4 slices broken cooked bacon**, and **sliced pickled okra**.

6 SMOKED TROUT & APPLE

Top **16 toasted baguette slices** with ½ **cup crème fraîche, 8 ounces flaked smoked trout, ¼ cup sliced apple, 2 tablespoons dill**, and a drizzle of **lemon juice**.

7 BLUE CHEESE & DATE

Top **16 baguette slices** with **6 ounces blue cheese** and **8 chopped pitted dates**. Broil until melted. Top with **honey** and **sliced chives**.

8 SPICY PEA & FETA

Mash together **2 cups cooked peas, 4 teaspoons olive oil, 1 tablespoon finely grated lemon zest**, and **kosher salt**. Top **16 toasted baguette slices** with the mashed peas, **4 ounces feta**, and **pepper flakes**.

9 MISO BUTTER & RADISH

Combine **4 tablespoons butter** and **1 tablespoon miso**. Top **16 toasted baguette slices** with the miso butter, **6 sliced radishes, 1 sliced scallion**, and **toasted sesame seeds**.

10 AVOCADO & OLIVE

Mash together **1 avocado** and **kosher salt**. Top **16 toasted baguette slices** with the mashed avocado, ⅓ **cup sliced olives, sambal**, and **lemon zest**.

11 ARTICHOKE & GRUYÈRE

Combine **4 ounces cream cheese, 2 ounces grated Gruyère, 2 tablespoons minced red onion**, and **kosher salt**. Spread on **16 baguette slices**. Broil until melted. Top with **4 quartered artichoke hearts**.

12 PROSCIUTTO & TOMATO

Top **16 toasted baguette slices** with ½ **cup mayonnaise, 16 sun-dried tomatoes, 4 ounces torn prosciutto, ½ cup arugula**, and **kosher salt**.

1 SPICY BLOODY MARY
MAKES *8 servings*
WORKING TIME *5 minutes*
TOTAL TIME *5 minutes*

Combine **46 ounces vegetable juice, 1 cup vodka,
2 tablespoons lemon juice,
2 tablespoons chopped dill,
1 tablespoon prepared horseradish, 1 tablespoon Worcestershire, 1 tablespoon hot sauce,** ¾ teaspoon black pepper, and ¾ **teaspoon celery seed.** Serve over ice with **dilly beans, lemon wedges,** and **celery**.

2 ROSEMARY-GRAPEFRUIT FIZZ
MAKES *8 servings*
WORKING TIME *5 minutes*
TOTAL TIME *15 minutes*

Simmer **4 sprigs rosemary,**
½ **cup sugar,** and ½ cup water until the sugar is dissolved; cool. Discard the rosemary. Combine the syrup, **1 liter seltzer, 3 cups grapefruit juice, 1½ cups vodka,** and a **dash of bitters.** Serve over ice with rosemary sprigs.

Deserve A Toast

Drinks That

Pair a by-the-batch cocktail with a red wine, a white wine, and a sparkling wine to round out your beverage selection.

③ LAMBRUSCO SANGRIA

MAKES *8 servings*
WORKING TIME *5 minutes*
TOTAL TIME *25 minutes*

Combine **1½ cups pear nectar**, **¾ cup Grand Marnier**, **1 cup halved grapes**, **1 sliced pear**, and **1 sliced lemon**; chill. Add **1 750-milliliter bottle Lambrusco wine**.

④ SLOW-COOKER APPLE CIDER

MAKES *8 servings*
WORKING TIME *5 minutes*
TOTAL TIME *4 hours, 5 minutes*

Combine **64 ounces apple cider, 6 chai tea bags, 2 cinnamon sticks**, and **1 split vanilla bean** in a slow cooker. Cook on low 3 to 4 hours. Discard the tea bags; stir in **¼ cup lemon juice**. Serve warm with **apple slices** and cinnamon sticks.

⑤ BOURBON NEGRONI

MAKES *1 serving*
WORKING TIME *5 minutes*
TOTAL TIME *5 minutes*

Combine **1½ ounces bourbon, ¾ ounce sweet vermouth, ¾ ounce Campari**, and ice in a cocktail shaker; shake 30 seconds. Serve with an **orange peel**.

⑥ GINGER & APPLE COOLER

MAKES *1 serving*
WORKING TIME *5 minutes*
TOTAL TIME *5 minutes*

Combine **2 tablespoons Calvados, 1 teaspoon maple syrup, 1 teaspoon lemon juice**, and ice in a cocktail shaker; shake 30 seconds. Serve topped with **wheat beer** or **ginger beer** and **candied ginger**.

⑦ BLOOD ORANGE MARGARITA

MAKES *1 serving*
WORKING TIME *5 minutes*
TOTAL TIME *5 minutes*

Muddle **2 jalapeño slices** and **3 sprigs cilantro** in a cocktail shaker. Add **1½ ounces tequila, ½ ounce lime juice**, and ice; shake 30 seconds. Serve topped with **blood orange soda**, jalapeño, and **cilantro**.

⑧ SPICED CRANBERRY PUNCH

MAKES *8 servings*
WORKING TIME *5 minutes*
TOTAL TIME *25 minutes*

Combine **6 cups cranberry juice cocktail, 1½ cups spiced rum, 1½ cups orange juice**, and **¼ cup lime juice**; chill. Serve with **cranberries**.

⑨ LIME GIMLET

MAKES *8 servings*
WORKING TIME *5 minutes*
TOTAL TIME *25 minutes*

Combine **3 cups seltzer, 1 cup gin, ½ cup simple syrup**, and **½ cup Key lime juice**; chill. Serve with **Key lime slices**.

savor

SHOWSTOPPING ENTREES

- - - - - - - - - - - - -

Everyone's got that family member who's not coming over for Christmas dinner unless there's a turkey. (And maybe that family member is you.) But that doesn't mean you can't give an old bird a new twist—whether that means a slew of unexpected garnishes or a walk on the fried side—or double up with an additional, complementary main dish.

Roasted, deep-fried, or rolled up into a roulade, everybody's favorite bird comes in an array of delightful configurations. For this spiced-up variety, turn to page 242.

SALT & PEPPER TURKEY

MAKES *8 servings (with leftovers)*
WORKING TIME *10 minutes*
TOTAL TIME *3 hours, 40 minutes*

2 carrots, halved
2 celery ribs, halved
1 onion, quartered
1 (12-pound) turkey, giblets discarded
4 tablespoons unsalted butter, softened
   Kosher salt and black pepper

1. Preheat the oven to 350°F. Place the carrots, celery, onion, and 2 cups of water in a roasting pan; top with a roasting rack.

2. Loosen the skin on the turkey breasts, starting at the neck, and rub the butter under the skin. Season the turkey (including the cavity) with 2 teaspoons salt and 1 teaspoon pepper; place on the roasting rack. Tie the legs together with kitchen twine and tuck the wings under.

3. Roast, basting every 30 minutes and tenting with foil if the skin becomes too dark, until the internal temperature (in the thickest part of the thigh) reaches 165°F, 2½ to 3 hours.

4. Gently tilt the turkey to release the juices from the cavity into the pan. Transfer the turkey to a cutting board; rest for at least 30 minutes before carving.

5. Scrape up the brown bits from the bottom of the pan and transfer, along with vegetables and pan juices, to a large, straight-sided skillet; reserve.

Go-To
5 Gravy Upgrades

| №1 |

Bay Leaf, Beer, & Orange Gravy

MAKES *8 servings*
WORKING TIME *5 minutes*
TOTAL TIME *45 minutes*

Reserved vegetables and pan juices from Salt and Pepper Turkey
2 bay leaves
½ cup stout beer
½ cup orange juice
¼ cup all-purpose flour
4 cups chicken stock
Black pepper

1. Cook the reserved vegetables, pan juices, and bay leaves in a large, straight-sided skillet over medium-high heat, stirring occasionally, until dark brown and thickened, 14 to 16 minutes. Add the beer and orange juice, and simmer, stirring occasionally, until syrupy, 6 to 8 minutes.

2. Sprinkle the flour into the skillet and cook, stirring, 30 seconds. Stir in the stock and simmer, stirring occasionally, until thickened, 14 to 16 minutes. Strain through a fine-mesh sieve. Season with pepper.

| №2 |

Thyme & Apple Cider Gravy

MAKES *8 servings*
WORKING TIME *5 minutes*
TOTAL TIME *45 minutes*

Reserved vegetables and pan juices from Salt and Pepper Turkey
2 thyme sprigs
½ cup apple cider
¼ cup all-purpose flour
4 cups chicken stock
Black pepper

1. Cook the reserved vegetables, pan juices, and thyme in a large, straight-sided skillet over medium-high heat, stirring occasionally, until dark brown and thickened, 14 to 16 minutes. Add the cider and simmer, stirring occasionally, until syrupy, 6 to 8 minutes.

2. Sprinkle the flour into the skillet and cook, stirring, 30 seconds. Stir in the stock and simmer, stirring occasionally, until thickened, 14 to 16 minutes. Strain through a fine-mesh sieve. Season with pepper.

| № 3 |

Shallot, Cognac, & Cream Gravy

MAKES *8 servings*
WORKING TIME *5 minutes*
TOTAL TIME *45 minutes*

Reserved vegetables and pan juices from Salt and Pepper Turkey
1 shallot, chopped
½ cup cognac
¼ cup all-purpose flour
4 cups chicken stock
¼ cup heavy cream
Black pepper

1. Cook the reserved vegetables, pan juices, and shallot in a large, straight-sided skillet over medium-high heat, stirring occasionally, until dark brown and thickened, 14 to 16 minutes. Add the cognac and simmer, stirring occasionally, until syrupy, 6 to 8 minutes.

2. Sprinkle the flour into skillet and cook, stirring, 30 seconds. Stir in the stock and simmer, stirring occasionally, until thickened, 14 to 16 minutes. Add the cream and simmer, until thickened, 3 to 4 minutes. Strain through a fine-mesh sieve. Season with pepper.

| № 4 |

Sage & Pomegranate Juice Gravy

MAKES *8 servings*
WORKING TIME *5 minutes*
TOTAL TIME *45 minutes*

Reserved vegetables and pan juices from Salt and Pepper Turkey
2 sprigs sage
½ cup dry white wine
¼ cup pomegranate juice
¼ cup all-purpose flour
4 cups chicken stock
Black pepper

1. Cook the reserved vegetables, pan juices, and sage in a large, straight-sided skillet over medium-high heat, stirring occasionally, until dark brown and thickened, 14 to 16 minutes. Add the wine and pomegranate juice and simmer, stirring occasionally, until syrupy, 6 to 8 minutes.

2. Sprinkle the flour into the skillet and cook, stirring, 30 seconds. Stir in the stock and simmer, stirring occasionally, until thickened, 14 to 16 minutes. Strain through a fine-mesh sieve. Season with pepper.

| № 5 |

Rosemary & Bourbon Gravy

MAKES *8 servings*
WORKING TIME *5 minutes*
TOTAL TIME *45 minutes*

Reserved vegetables and pan juices from Salt and Pepper Turkey
2 sprigs rosemary
½ cup bourbon
¼ cup all-purpose flour
4 cups chicken stock
Black pepper

1. Cook the reserved vegetables, pan juices, and rosemary in a large, straight-sided skillet over medium-high heat, stirring occasionally, until dark brown and thickened, 14 to 16 minutes. Add the bourbon and simmer, stirring occasionally, until syrupy, 6 to 8 minutes.

2. Sprinkle the flour into the skillet and cook, stirring, 30 seconds. Stir in the stock and simmer, stirring occasionally, until thickened, 14 to 16 minutes. Strain through a fine-mesh sieve. Season with pepper.

FRIED TURKEY

MAKES *10 to 12 servings*
WORKING TIME *1 hour, 35 minutes*
TOTAL TIME *2 hours*

1½ tablespoons kosher salt
1½ tablespoons smoked paprika
1½ teaspoons garlic powder
1½ teaspoons onion powder
1½ teaspoons freshly ground black pepper
1¼ teaspoons cayenne pepper
1 (12- to 14-pound) fresh whole turkey
Peanut oil (about 3 gallons)

TIP
If you have a crowd or want extra leftovers, you can fry an additional turkey in the same oil—just be sure to heat it back up to 350°F. Save your oil containers; they'll come in handy when it's time to clean up.

1. Stir together the salt, paprika, garlic powder, onion powder, black pepper, and cayenne pepper. Remove the giblets and neck from the turkey, and discard. Drain the cavity well; pat the entire turkey dry with paper towels. Loosen and lift the skin from the turkey with your fingers, without totally detaching the skin; generously spread about half of the seasoning mix under the skin. Carefully replace the skin and secure with wooden picks, if desired. Sprinkle and rub the remaining seasoning inside the cavity and on the outside of the turkey. Let the turkey stand at room temperature while the oil heats.

2. Meanwhile, pour the oil into a deep propane turkey fryer 10 to 12 inches from the top. Heat to 350°F over a medium-low flame, according to the manufacturer's instructions (about 45 minutes).

3. Place the turkey on the fryer rod. Carefully and slowly lower the turkey into hot oil with the rod attachment.

4. Fry 35 to 45 minutes or until a meat thermometer inserted in the thickest portion of the thigh registers 165°F (about 3 minutes per pound plus an additional 5 minutes. Keep the oil temperature between 300°F and 325°F). Remove the turkey from the oil; drain and let stand 25 minutes before slicing.

PICKLED PEACH & CRANBERRY
SALSA

MAKES *8 servings*
WORKING TIME *15 minutes*
TOTAL TIME *25 minutes*

1½ cups fresh cranberries, chopped

1 fresh jalapeño pepper, finely chopped

¼ cup finely chopped fresh cilantro

2 tablespoons sugar

1 teaspoon lime zest

1 tablespoon lime juice

¾ teaspoon finely grated fresh ginger

¼ teaspoon kosher salt

¼ teaspoon freshly ground pepper

¾ cup chopped pickled peaches

Stir together all the ingredients except the peaches in a medium bowl. Let stand 10 minutes, stirring occasionally. Fold in the peaches and season with additional salt and pepper to taste. Chill until ready to serve, up to 6 hours.

TURKEY ROULADE
THREE WAYS

MAKES *8 servings*
WORKING TIME *30 minutes*
TOTAL TIME *1 hour, 25 minutes*

- 2 boneless, skinless turkey breasts (3½ to 4 pounds total)
  Kosher salt and freshly ground black pepper
- 1 recipe Take-Your-Pick Filling (see page 246)
- 1½ tablespoons canola oil

1. Preheat the oven to 425°F. Line a rimmed baking sheet with foil and fit it with a wire rack.

2. Butterfly the breasts crosswise, being sure not to cut all the way through. Place a piece of plastic wrap over one open breast, and pound to a rectangle about 12×14 inches (¼ inch thick). Season with salt and pepper. Repeat with the remaining breast.

3. Spread half of the desired filling onto one breast, pressing to adhere. Tightly roll from one long side and secure with butcher's twine. Tuck the ends under and tie lengthwise with butcher's twine. Repeat with the remaining breast and filling. Rub the roulades with oil, dividing evenly. Season with salt and pepper.

4. Bake on the prepared baking sheet until an instant-read thermometer inserted in the thickest part reads 165°F, 40 to 45 minutes. Let stand 10 minutes before slicing.

Take-Your-Pick
3 Fillings

Each filling recipe makes enough for one roulade recipe.

| *No* 1 |

Fennel-Apple

Cook **1 chopped fennel bulb**, **2 chopped Honeycrisp apples**, and **2 chopped shallots** in 2 tablespoons unsalted butter in a large skillet over medium heat, stirring occasionally, until golden brown, 10 to 12 minutes. Stir in **2 tablespoons chopped fresh tarragon** and **2 tablespoons fennel fronds**. Season with kosher salt and freshly ground black pepper.

| *No* 2 |

Sausage-Cornbread

Cook **8 ounces Italian sausage** (casing removed) in a large skillet over medium-high heat, breaking it up into small pieces with a wooden spoon, until no longer pink, 5 to 7 minutes. Stir in **2 minced garlic cloves**; cook 1 minute. Add **2 cups crumbled cornbread** and **1 tablespoon chopped fresh thyme**. Remove from the heat, and stir in ½ **cup chicken stock**. Season with kosher salt and freshly ground black pepper.

| *No* 3 |

Bacon-Mushroom

Cook **4 slices chopped thick-cut bacon** in a large skillet over medium heat until crisp, 6 to 8 minutes. Remove to a plate with a slotted spoon; pour off all but 1½ tablespoons drippings. Add **1 pound chopped assorted mushrooms** to the drippings; cook, stirring occasionally, until lightly browned, 8 to 10 minutes. Add **1 bunch chopped scallions** and ⅓ **cup chopped fresh flat-leaf parsley**; cook, stirring occasionally, until the scallions are tender, about 2 minutes. Stir in ¼ **cup dry white wine**; cook until the wine evaporates, 3 to 4 minutes. Stir in **3 tablespoons seasoned bread crumbs**. Season with kosher salt and freshly ground black pepper.

HOW TO
roll a roulade

1 Butterfly the turkey breast crosswise, being sure not to cut all the way through. Open like a book.

2 Place a piece of plastic wrap over one breast and pound (using a meat mallet or rolling pin). Repeat with remaining breast.

3 Place 5 (10-inch) pieces of butcher's twine under the breast, spacing evenly. Spread the filling on the breast, pressing to help adhere. Tightly roll up the breast.

4 Tie the twine, and trim the excess. Tuck the ends under. Tie 1 (25-inch) piece of twine lengthwise to help secure.

SWEET ONION & HERB
GRAVY

MAKES *3 cups*
WORKING TIME *1 hour*
TOTAL TIME *1 hour, 10 minutes*

- 6 tablespoons unsalted butter
- 1 sweet onion, chopped
- 2 garlic cloves, chopped
- ⅓ cup all-purpose flour
- 6 cups chicken stock
- ¾ cup dry white wine
- 2 tablespoons chopped fresh flat-leaf parsley
- 2 tablespoons chopped fresh chives
- 1 tablespoon chopped fresh thyme
  Kosher salt and freshly ground black pepper

1. Melt the butter in a large straight-sided skillet over medium-high heat. Add the onion, and cook, stirring occasionally, until golden brown, 10 to 12 minutes. Add the garlic, and cook 1 minute. Sprinkle the flour over the onion, and cook, whisking, until the flour is golden brown, 1 minute.

2. Slowly whisk in the stock and wine. Cook, whisking often, until reduced to 3 cups or until the gravy reaches desired thickness, 45 to 50 minutes.

3. Strain through a fine-mesh sieve; discard solids. Stir in the parsley, chives, and thyme. Season with salt and pepper.

SLOE GIN
HAM

Finish up to 2 days ahead, cool, then chill (loosely wrapped in foil). Any leftovers will keep well in the fridge for up to four days.

MAKES *8 servings, with leftovers*
WORKING TIME *25 minutes, plus cooling*
TOTAL TIME *about 4 hours, 55 minutes*

Whole boneless smoked or unsmoked ham, about 9 pounds
1 liter apple juice
1 onion, sliced
2 bay leaves
1 cinnamon stick
20 or so peppercorns
40 to 50 whole cloves

For the glaze
3½ ounces plum jam
2½ tablespoons sugar
3 ounces sloe gin

1. Weigh the ham, put it into a large deep pan, and add the apple juice. Fill with cold water to cover; add the onion, bay leaves, cinnamon, and peppercorns. Bring to boil, reduce the heat, cover, and simmer for 25 minutes per pound until cooked through, skimming the surface regularly (to reduce saltiness) if you're saving the juices to use for stock at a later date.

2. Remove the ham from the cooking liquid and put on a board. Leave to cool for 15 minutes.

3. Preheat the oven to 425°F. Untie the ham; use a knife to remove the skin, leaving a good layer of fat on the ham. Score a diamond pattern into the fat (not cutting down into meat). Retie the ham (to maintain a better shape) and stud a clove into each diamond.

4. Line a roasting pan that will just fit the ham with a double layer of foil. Add the ham (fat-side up). In a small bowl, mix the glaze ingredients. Brush roughly half over the meat and into the fat. Roast 25 to 30 minutes, basting with the rest of glaze every 10 minutes, until the skin is caramelized. Slice and serve warm or at room temperature.

CHOUX CROWN

Add some pancetta to the pan along with the mushrooms if you want to include a meat element.

MAKES *4 servings as a main, or 8 as a side*
WORKING TIME *35 minutes, plus cooling*
TOTAL TIME *1 hour, 20 minutes*

- 5 tablespoons butter, chilled and cut into small cubes, plus extra to grease the pan
- 3 large eggs, divided
- 7/8 cup all-purpose flour
- 3/4 teaspoon English mustard powder
- 2 ounces Gruyère cheese, grated
- Salt and pepper, to taste
- Poppy seeds, to sprinkle

For the filling
- 2 tablespoons butter
- 2 large shallots, finely sliced
- 13 ounces chestnut mushrooms, sliced
- 3 ounces dry sherry, optional
- 3½ ounces crème fraîche
- 4 ounces double cream
- Large handful parsley, finely chopped
- Zest of ½ lemon, finely grated
- 2 ounces watercress, roughly chopped
- ½ ounce dried cranberries, chopped

1. Preheat the oven to 400°F and grease a large baking sheet. Put the butter and 7/8 cup cold water into a medium pan. Beat 2 of the eggs together in a bowl. Heat the butter mixture, stirring to melt. Turn up the heat and, as soon as the mixture comes to a boil, take the pan off the heat, add the flour, and beat until the mixture comes away from the sides of the pan and is glossy—about 30 seconds. Set aside to cool for 10 minutes.

2. Gradually mix in the beaten eggs, mixing well after each addition. Add the mustard powder and cheese, and season to taste. Mix to combine. Scrape the mixture into a piping bag fitted with a ½-inch plain nozzle. Onto the prepared sheet, pipe an 8-inch circle, squeezing out plenty of mixture so the ring is about ¾ inch wide and ¾ inch deep. With the remaining mixture, pipe 8 small mounds on top of the ring, spacing evenly apart (to resemble a crown). Using a damp finger, smooth the ring and mounds. Lightly beat remaining egg and brush over the ring and mounds. Sprinkle on the poppy seeds.

3. Bake for 30 minutes until well risen and deeply golden. Carefully remove the baking sheet and pierce a few steam holes into the sides of the ring. Return to the oven for 10 minutes.

4. Meanwhile, make the filling. Melt the butter in a large frying pan and gently cook shallots for 5 minutes to soften. Turn up heat to high and add mushrooms. Fry, stirring occasionally, until tender and there's no liquid left in pan. Add sherry, if using, and bubble until pan is again almost dry. Stir in the crème fraîche and double cream and bubble to thicken, about 5 minutes.

5. Transfer the warm choux ring to a cake stand or board. Carefully slice off the top third. Mix the parsley, lemon zest, and watercress into the mushroom mixture and adjust the salt and pepper to taste. Spoon the filling into the base layer of the ring and sprinkle the cranberries over top. Top with the remaining choux layer and serve.

taste

DISPLAY-WORTHY DESSERTS

- - - - - - - - - - -

From cakes so ornate they could stand in for centerpieces to pies that will have Grandma inquiring about the recipe, make the last thing they eat the thing they'll remember the longest.

Turn to pages 266–269 for recipes to create these delicious seasonal pies.

BASIC PIE DOUGH

MAKES *8 servings*
WORKING TIME *10 minutes*
TOTAL TIME *2 hours, 10 minutes*

- 2½ cups all-purpose flour, spooned and leveled
- 1 teaspoon kosher salt
- 1 teaspoon sugar
- 1 cup (2 sticks) cold unsalted butter, cut up
- ¼ cup ice water

1. Whisk together the flour, salt, and sugar. Cut in the butter until it resembles coarse meal with several pea-size pieces remaining. Add the water, 1 tablespoon at a time, using a fork to pull the dough together into a crumbly pile (add up to an additional 2 tablespoons of water if needed).

2. Divide the dough into two piles; wrap each in plastic wrap. Use the plastic to flatten and press the dough into disks. Refrigerate until firm, 2 hours.

APPLE-RASPBERRY
PIE

MAKES *8 servings*
WORKING TIME *25 minutes*
TOTAL TIME *5 hours, 55 minutes*

- 2 tablespoons all-purpose flour, plus more for surface
- 1 recipe Basic Pie Dough
- ¼ cup raspberry jam
- 2 tablespoons sugar
- 1 teaspoon pure vanilla extract
- ¼ teaspoon kosher salt
- 2½ pounds Granny Smith, Golden Delicious, or Pink Lady apples, peeled and thinly sliced
- 1 cup frozen raspberries
- 1 egg
- Raw sugar, for sprinkling

1. Preheat the oven to 350°F. On a floured surface, roll one disk of dough into a 13-inch circle. Transfer to a 9-inch pie plate; trim the overhang to 1 inch.

2. Whisk together the flour, jam, sugar, vanilla, and salt. Add the apples and raspberries; toss to coat. Transfer to the pie plate. Freeze for 15 minutes.

3. While the pie is in the freezer, crack the egg in a small bowl and add 2 tablespoons of water. Beat egg until well combined. Set aside to use as egg wash on pie dough.

4. On a floured surface, roll the remaining disk of dough into a 13-inch circle. Cut into 1½-inch strips; discard trimmings. Weave the strips into a lattice pattern over the fruit. Fold the bottom overhang over the lattice edges and crimp to seal. Brush the dough with the egg wash; sprinkle with raw sugar. Freeze 15 minutes.

5. Bake, on a baking sheet, until golden and bubbling, 60 to 75 minutes. Cool, on a rack, at least 4 hours.

Clockwise from top: Apple-Raspberry Pie, Caramelized Apple Cheesecake, Brown Butter–Apple Pie with Cheddar Crust, and Ginger-Apple-Walnut Crumble Pie

CARAMELIZED APPLE
CHEESECAKE

MAKES *8 servings*
WORKING TIME *30 minutes*
TOTAL TIME *3 hours, 30 minutes*

14 graham crackers

⅔ cup plus 1 tablespoon sugar, divided

¾ teaspoon kosher salt, divided

½ cup unsalted butter, melted

16 ounces cream cheese, at room temperature

⅓ cup sour cream, at room temperature

1 vanilla bean, seeds scraped

2 large eggs, at room temperature

2 large apples, peeled and sliced

1. Preheat the oven to 325°F. Pulse the graham crackers, 1 tablespoon of the sugar, and ½ teaspoon of the salt in a food processor until fine crumbs form, 8 to 10 times. Add the butter and pulse to combine, 4 to 6 times. Press the mixture into the bottom and up the sides of a 9-inch pie plate. Bake until set, 12 to 15 minutes; cool.

2. Pulse the cream cheese, ⅓ cup of the sugar, and the remaining ¼ teaspoon of salt in a food processor, until smooth, 8 to 10 times. Add the sour cream and vanilla seeds; pulse until smooth, 3 to 4 times. Scrape down the sides of the bowl, add the eggs, and pulse to combine; pour into the crust. Bake until edges are set but center is still wobbly, 30 to 35 minutes. Cool on a rack. Chill at least 2 hours.

3. Melt the remaining ⅓ cup of sugar in a large skillet over medium heat. Add the apples and cook, stirring, until golden, 10 to 12 minutes. Stir in 3 tablespoons water and cook, stirring, until smooth and slightly reduced, 1 to 2 minutes; cool. Spoon over the cheesecake.

BROWN BUTTER–APPLE PIE
WITH CHEDDAR CRUST

MAKES *8 servings*
WORKING TIME *25 minutes*
TOTAL TIME *5 hours, 40 minutes*

- 1 recipe Basic Pie Dough (see step 1)
- 4 ounces sharp Cheddar cheese, grated
- 3 tablespoons all-purpose flour, plus more for surface
- 4 tablespoons unsalted butter
- ⅓ cup packed light brown sugar
- ½ teaspoon ground cinnamon
- ¾ teaspoon kosher salt
- 2½ pounds Granny smith, Golden Delicious, or Pink Lady apples, peeled and thinly sliced
- 1 egg

1. Make the dough as instructed, tossing the cheese into the flour mixture before adding the butter.

2. Preheat the oven to 350°F. On a floured surface, roll one disk of the dough into a 13-inch circle. Transfer to a 9-inch pie plate.

3. Cook the butter in a small saucepan over medium heat, swirling, until golden brown, 2 to 4 minutes. Whisk together the flour, brown sugar, cinnamon, and salt. Add the apples and brown butter; toss to coat. Transfer to the pie plate.

4. On a floured surface, roll the remaining disk of dough into a 13-inch circle. Place on the pie; trim overhang to 1 inch. Tuck the overhangs underneath and crimp; cut four vents in the top crust. Freeze 15 minutes.

5. While the pie is in the freezer, crack the egg in a small bowl and add 2 tablespoons of water. Beat egg until well combined. Set aside to use as egg wash on pie dough.

6. Remove the pie from the freezer. Brush with the egg. Bake, on a baking sheet, until golden and bubbling, 60 to 75 minutes. Cool, on a rack, at least 4 hours.

GINGER-APPLE-WALNUT
CRUMBLE PIE

MAKES *8 servings*
WORKING TIME *25 minutes*
TOTAL TIME *5 hours, 35 minutes*

- 1¼ cups plus 2 tablespoons all-purpose flour, divided, plus more for surface
- ½ recipe Basic Pie Dough
- ⅓ cup sugar
- ½ teaspoon ground cinnamon
- 2½ tablespoons grated fresh ginger, divided
- ½ teaspoon kosher salt, divided
- 2½ pounds Granny Smith, Golden Delicious, or Pink Lady apples, peeled and cut into 1-inch pieces
- ¾ cup chopped walnuts
- ½ cup packed light brown sugar
- ½ cup unsalted butter, at room temperature

1. Preheat the oven to 350°F. On a floured surface, roll the dough into a 13-inch circle. Transfer to a 9-inch pie plate, fold the edges under, and align with the rim of the plate; crimp.

2. Whisk together the sugar, cinnamon, 2 tablespoons of the flour, 1½ tablespoons of the ginger, and ¼ teaspoon of the salt. Add the apples; toss to coat. Transfer to the pie plate. Freeze for 15 minutes.

3. Whisk together the walnuts, brown sugar, remaining 1¼ cups of flour, remaining 1 tablespoon of ginger, and remaining ¼ teaspoon of salt. Work in the butter until large clumps form; crumble over the apples.

4. Bake, on a baking sheet, until golden and bubbling, 60 to 70 minutes (tent with foil if the crumble becomes too dark). Cool, on a rack, at least 4 hours.

PUMPKIN PIE
WITH
OAT-PECAN CRUST

MAKES *8 servings*
WORKING TIME *25 minutes*
TOTAL TIME *4 hours, 50 minutes*

- 2 cups pecans
- 1 cup old-fashioned rolled oats
- 4 tablespoons unsalted butter, melted
- 2 tablespoons sugar
- ¾ teaspoon kosher salt, divided
- 1 cup pure pumpkin puree
- ½ cup heavy cream
- ⅓ cup packed light brown sugar
- ¼ cup whole milk
- 2 large eggs plus 1 large egg white
- ½ teaspoon ground cinnamon
- ½ teaspoon ground ginger
- Pinch ground cloves
- Candied pecans, for serving

1. Preheat the oven to 350°F. Toast the pecans and oats on a baking sheet until golden and fragrant, 10 to 12 minutes; cool.

2. Process the pecans, oats, butter, sugar, and ½ teaspoon of the salt in a food processor until finely ground, 2 to 4 minutes. Press the mixture into the bottom and up the sides of a 9-inch pie plate. Freeze 15 minutes. Bake, on a baking sheet, until set, 20 to 25 minutes. Cool on a rack.

3. Whisk together pumpkin, cream, brown sugar, milk, eggs, cinnamon, ginger, cloves, and remaining ¼ teaspoon of salt. Pour into the crust and bake until the filling is set, 40 to 45 minutes. Cool on a rack. Chill at least 2 hours.

4. Serve topped with candied pecans.

BOURBON-PECAN

PIE

MAKES *8 to 10 servings*
WORKING TIME *35 minutes*
TOTAL TIME *2 hours, 25 minutes*

For the crust

- 2 cups all-purpose flour, spooned and leveled, plus more for work surface
- 2 tablespoons sugar
- ½ teaspoon kosher salt
- ¾ cup (1½ sticks) cold unsalted butter, cut into cubes
- 3 tablespoons ice water

For the filling

- ½ cup (1 stick) unsalted butter, at room temperature
- 1 cup sugar
- 2 large eggs, lightly beaten
- ½ cup all-purpose flour, spooned and leveled
- 2 tablespoons bourbon
- ⅛ teaspoon kosher salt
- 1 cup chopped pecans, more for serving
- 1 cup semisweet chocolate chips
- Whipped cream and chocolate shavings, for serving

1. To make the crust, preheat the oven to 350°F. Pulse the flour, sugar, and salt in a food processor until combined, 2 to 3 times. Add the butter and pulse until the mixture resembles coarse meal, 10 to 12 times. Add the water, 1 tablespoon at a time, and pulse until large clumps form (add up to 2 additional tablespoons of water if needed). Gather the dough into a ball, and roll into a ¾-inch-thick disk. Wrap in plastic wrap; chill 30 minutes.

2. On a floured work surface, roll the dough into a 13-inch round. Transfer to a 9-inch pie plate; fold the edges under to align with the rim of the plate; crimp. Freeze for 30 minutes. Line the pie plate over the crust with parchment paper and fill with pie weights or dried beans. Bake until golden brown, 15 to 20 minutes. Remove the pie weights and parchment and cool.

3. To make the filling, beat the butter and sugar with an electric mixer on medium speed until combined, 1 to 2 minutes. Add the eggs, flour, bourbon, and salt and beat to combine, about 1 minute. Fold in the pecans and chocolate chips. Transfer to the parbaked pie crust, and bake until the center is set, 30 to 35 minutes. Cool completely on a wire rack.

4. Serve topped with whipped cream, chopped pecans, and chocolate shavings.

Opposite, clockwise from top left: Bourbon-Pecan Pie, Dark Chocolate–Pecan Toffee, Pecan Shortbread Cookies, and Pumpkin-Pecan Bread Pudding

DARK CHOCOLATE– PECAN TOFFEE

MAKES *8 to 10 servings*
WORKING TIME *25 minutes*
TOTAL TIME *1 hour, 25 minutes*

- 1 cup (2 sticks) unsalted butter, cut up, plus more for baking sheet
- 1½ cups pecan halves, divided
- ¾ cup sugar
- ¼ cup packed light brown sugar
- ½ teaspoon kosher salt
- ½ teaspoon pure vanilla extract
- 1 (3.5-ounce) dark chocolate bar, chopped
- ¾ teaspoon large flaked sea salt (such as Maldon)

1. Preheat the oven to 350°F. Butter a rimmed baking sheet.

2. Spread the pecans on a second rimmed baking sheet and toast just until fragrant, 7 to 8 minutes; cool. Arrange 1 cup of the toasted pecans, flat side down, in a single layer on the buttered baking sheet, leaving a 2- to 3-inch border along the sides. Chop the remaining ½ cup pecans; set aside.

3. Combine the butter, sugar, brown sugar, salt, vanilla, and ¼ cup water in a medium saucepan. Cook over medium-low heat, stirring constantly, until the mixture reaches 290°F, 18 to 20 minutes. Slowly pour the hot caramel mixture over the pecans, making sure to fully cover each nut and leaving the 2- to 3-inch border around the baking sheet.

4. Sprinkle the chocolate evenly over the toffee; let sit until slightly melted. Spread the chocolate in an even layer. Sprinkle with the chopped pecans and sea salt. Let stand 20 minutes, then refrigerate until cool and set, 40 to 45 minutes. Break into small pieces.

PECAN SHORTBREAD COOKIES

MAKES *36 cookies*
WORKING TIME *40 minutes*
TOTAL TIME *2 hours, 20 minutes*

- 3 cups pecan halves, divided
- 1 cup (2 sticks) unsalted butter, at room temperature
- ½ cup sugar
- 1 teaspoon pure vanilla extract
- ½ teaspoon kosher salt
- 2¼ cups all-purpose flour, spooned and leveled
- ½ cup turbinado sugar

1. Preheat the oven to 350°F. Line two baking sheets with parchment. Spread 2 cups of the pecans on a rimmed baking sheet and toast just until fragrant, 7 to 8 minutes. Cool, then chop.

2. Beat the butter, sugar, vanilla, and salt with an electric mixer on medium speed until light and fluffy, 1 to 2 minutes. Reduce the speed to low and beat in the flour, one large spoonful at a time, just until combined. Add the chopped pecans and beat until incorporated. Cover and chill at least 1 hour, up to 24 hours.

3. Place the turbinado sugar in a bowl. Divide the dough into 36 (1¼-inch) balls. Roll the balls in the turbinado sugar, and place, 2 inches apart, on the prepared baking sheets. Gently press one of the remaining pecans into the top of each cookie. Bake, rotating the pans once, until the edges are golden brown, 15 to 17 minutes. Cool on the pans on wire racks 5 minutes, then transfer to the racks to cool completely.

PUMPKIN-PECAN
BREAD PUDDING

MAKES *8 servings*
WORKING TIME *25 minutes*
TOTAL TIME *1 hour*

For the bread pudding

- Cooking spray
- ¾ cup pure pumpkin puree
- 2 large eggs
- 1 cup milk
- ½ cup heavy cream
- ½ cup packed dark brown sugar
- 4 tablespoons (½ stick) unsalted butter, melted
- 1 teaspoon ground cinnamon
- ½ teaspoon pure vanilla extract
- ½ teaspoon kosher salt
- ¼ teaspoon ground ginger
- ¼ teaspoon ground nutmeg
- 7 cups day-old brioche, cut into 1-inch cubes
- ½ cup pecan halves, roughly chopped

For the bourbon sauce

- 1 cup sugar
- ½ cup heavy cream
- 1 tablespoon bourbon

1. Preheat the oven to 350°F with the rack in the middle position. Spray an 8-by-8-inch baking dish with cooking spray.

2. To make the bread pudding, whisk together the pumpkin, eggs, milk, cream, brown sugar, butter, cinnamon, vanilla, salt, ginger, and nutmeg in a bowl until smooth. Fold in the bread and pecans. Let stand 30 minutes. Transfer to the prepared baking dish and bake until set, 30 to 35 minutes.

3. To make the bourbon sauce, combine the sugar and ¼ cup water in a medium saucepan. Bring to a boil over medium-high heat and cook, without stirring, until the sugar mixture is dark amber in color, 12 to 15 minutes. Remove from the heat and carefully add the cream and bourbon, stirring until smooth and creamy.

4. Serve the pudding with the sauce alongside.

GRAPE SLAB
PIE

MAKES *8 servings*
WORKING TIME *25 minutes*
TOTAL TIME *3 hours (not including pie crust)*

4 recipes Basic Pie Dough
　 All-purpose flour, for work surface
⅔ cup sugar
¼ cup cornstarch
1 tablespoon chopped fresh rosemary
1 teaspoon finely grated lemon zest
½ teaspoon kosher salt
¼ teaspoon freshly ground black pepper
3½ pounds seedless black grapes
1 tablespoon lemon juice
1 large egg, lightly beaten with
　 1 teaspoon water, to make a wash
3 tablespoons turbinado sugar
　 Pie Crust Leaves, for garnish
　 (see step 5)

1. Preheat the oven to 350°F. Press 2 disks of the dough together. On a lightly floured surface, roll the dough into a 15×20-inch rectangle. Transfer to a jelly roll pan and trim to a 1-inch overhang, reserving the trimmings. Refrigerate 15 minutes.

2. Whisk together the sugar, cornstarch, rosemary, lemon zest, salt, and pepper in a bowl. Add the grapes and toss to coat. Add the lemon juice and toss to combine. Transfer the grape mixture to the bottom crust and refrigerate while you roll out the top crust.

3. Press the remaining 2 disks of dough together. On a lightly floured surface, roll the remaining dough into a 15-by-20-inch rectangle. Cut the dough on the diagonal into 2-inch-thick strips. Lay the strips diagonally across top of pie, pressing to seal at the edges. Reserve any dough scraps. Freeze 15 minutes.

4. Brush the top of the pie dough with the egg wash and sprinkle with the turbinado sugar. Bake until the filling is bubbling and the crust is golden brown, 60 to 70 minutes. Cool on a wire rack.

5. Garnish with Pie Crust Leaves. To make, cut leaves from pie dough scraps with leaf-shaped cookie cutters. Bake at 350°F until golden.

Opposite, clockwise from top right: Grape Slab Pie, Maple-Nut Pie, and Apple Blossom Tart

PEPPERMINT ICEBOX
PIE

MAKES *8 servings*
WORKING TIME *40 minutes*
TOTAL TIME *4 hours*

For the crust
- 25 chocolate Oreo® cookies
- ¼ teaspoon kosher salt
- 5 tablespoons unsalted butter, melted

For the filling
- 12 ounces cream cheese, at room temperature
- 1 (7½-ounce) container marshmallow creme
- 1 tablespoon peppermint extract
- 1½ cups heavy cream
- ¾ cup confectioners' sugar
- 6 drops red food coloring

For the topping
- 1 cup heavy cream
- ¼ cup confectioners' sugar
- Crushed peppermint hard candies

1. Make the crust: Pulse the cookies in a food processor until fine crumbs form, 10 to 15 times. Add the salt and butter, and pulse to combine, 8 to 10 times. Press the crumb mixture into a 9-inch pie plate.

2. Make the filling: Beat the cream cheese with an electric mixer on medium speed until smooth, 2 to 3 minutes. Add the marshmallow creme and peppermint extract, and beat until combined. In a separate bowl, beat the cream and sugar with an electric mixer on high speed until very stiff peaks form, 1 to 2 minutes. Gently fold the cream mixture into cream cheese mixture. Gently fold in the food coloring. (For swirls, add a few extra drops of food coloring before spooning the filling into the pie crust; do not mix in—just stir once and then spoon it out of the bowl.) Spoon the filling into prepared crust. Cover and chill at least 3 hours, up to overnight.

3. Make the topping: Whip the cream and sugar with an electric mixer on high speed until soft peaks form, 1 to 2 minutes; spoon over the pie.

4. Garnish with crushed peppermints.

STAINED GLASS
CAKE

MAKES *12 servings*
WORKING TIME *1 hour, 30 minutes*
TOTAL TIME *2 hours*

1 recipe Chocolate Chip Cake
   (see page 273)
1 recipe White Vanilla Frosting
   (see page 141)
24 pink and red candies
   Pink sanding sugar

TIP
Melted Jolly Rancher® candies become the perfect "panes" for this stained-glass-inspired dessert.

1. Make the cake according to the recipe. Trim the domed tops of two of the layers. Place one trimmed layer on a cake stand or serving platter and top with ⅔ cup frosting. Repeat two more times, using the domed layer on top. Frost the top and sides with the remaining frosting.

2. Preheat the oven to 325°F. Line a baking pan with parchment paper. Line up three candies end to end in the one corner of the prepared baking pan. Repeat three more times in the remaining corners. Bake until the candy has melted together and makes one long piece, 3 to 5 minutes. Cool until cool enough to handle, 3 to 5 minutes; transfer to a lightly greased wire rack to cool completely. Repeat the process with the remaining 12 candies.

3. Gently tap the cooled candy on the edge of the baking sheet to crack it into shards. Brush the edges of the shards with water and dip into sanding sugar. Attach around the sides of the cake.

PINE TREE

CAKE

MAKES *12 servings*
WORKING TIME *1 hour, 20 minutes*
TOTAL TIME *2 hours, 30 minutes*

- 1 recipe Chocolate Chip Cake (see page 273)
- 1 recipe White Vanilla Frosting (see page 141)
- 1½ cups white nonpareils
- 1 cup large flake coconut
- ½ cup each green, vibrant green, blue, and turquoise candy melts
- 12 (6-inch) bamboo skewers
  White sprinkles
  Crushed white rock candy

1. Make the cake according to the recipe. Trim the domed tops of two of the layers. Place one trimmed layer on a cake stand or serving platter and top with ⅔ cup frosting. Repeat, then place the domed layer on top. Frost the sides with 1⅓ cups frosting; leave the top unfrosted. Chill for 30 minutes.

2. Spread the nonpareils on a small rimmed baking sheet. Carefully lift the cake from the top and bottom and roll the sides in nonpareils to coat. Return the cake to the cake stand or serving platter and frost the top with the remaining frosting. Sprinkle the coconut on top.

3. Melt the candy melts in separate glass bowls in the microwave. Mix together some of the colors to make different shades of green and greenish blue. Spoon the colors into separate small zip-top bags and snip a ⅛-inch hole in one corner of each bag.

4. Place the bamboo skewers, 3 inches apart, on parchment-lined baking sheets. Working in a back-and-forth motion, drizzle the melts over the skewers to create trees (be sure to leave 3 inches of the skewer uncovered). Repeat with all colors until you have 12 trees, all different sizes and colors.

5. Immediately decorate the trees with white sprinkles and rock candy. Chill until set, 25 to 30 minutes.

6. Gently lift the trees from the parchment and insert the skewers into the cake to create a forest.

HOW TO MAKE

pine trees

1 Fill zip-top bags with the melted candy melts. Snip a small hole in the corner of each bag.

2 Lay the bamboo skewers on a parchment paper-lined baking sheet and drizzle with melted candy melts to create tree shape. (Create different sizes and colors for a simple yet impressive display.)

3 Decorate the trees with candy.

4 Allow the trees to set, about 30 minutes, then gently peel from the parchment. Place the skewers in the cake.

CANDIED PRETZEL
CAKE

MAKES *12 servings*
WORKING TIME *2 hours*
TOTAL TIME *3 hours*

1 recipe Chocolate Chip Cake
  (see page 273)
1 recipe White Vanilla Frosting
  (see page 141)
35 large pretzel rods
2 (12-ounce) bags white candy melts
  (4 cups), melted
  Candy: blue and white sanding
  sugar; silver, white, and blue dragées;
  and crushed blue mint hard candies

1. Make the cake according to the recipe. Trim the domed tops of two of the layers. Place one trimmed layer on a cake stand or serving platter and top with ⅔ cup frosting. Repeat, then place the domed layer on top. Chill while decorating the pretzels.

2. Line a baking sheet with parchment paper. Trim the pretzel rods with a serrated knife so they will reach just above the top of the cake (about 4 inches total). Dip the cut end of one pretzel in melted candy melts, leaving the other end uncoated. Decorate with sanding sugar, dragées, and mints. Place on the prepared baking sheet. Repeat with the remaining pretzels, candy melts, and candy; reserve any unused candy melts. Let set at room temperature or in the fridge.

3. Attach the decorated pretzels around the sides of the cake.

4. Remelt the reserved candy melts. Spread in a thin layer, about ⅛ inch thick, on the back of a baking sheet. Chill until solid, 4 to 6 minutes. Use a flat metal spatula or bench scraper to scrape up the chocolate, creating curls and shards. Sprinkle over the top of the cake.

APPLE-CINNAMON LAYER CAKE
WITH SALTED CARAMEL FROSTING

MAKES *10 to 12 servings*
WORKING TIME *1 hour*
TOTAL TIME *1 hour, 40 minutes*

Cooking spray
¾ cup pecan halves
3 cups all-purpose flour, spooned and leveled
2½ teaspoons ground cinnamon
1 teaspoon kosher salt
1 teaspoon baking soda
½ teaspoon ground nutmeg
¼ teaspoon ground allspice
½ cup sugar
1 cup packed light brown sugar
3 large eggs
¾ cup canola oil
¾ cup unsweetened applesauce
1 teaspoon pure vanilla extract
4 cups diced peeled apples, such as Pink Lady or Granny Smith (from 2 large apples)
Salted Caramel Frosting (see facing page)
Candied pecans, for garnish

1. Preheat the oven to 350°F. Spray 3 (9-inch) round cake pans with cooking spray and line the bottoms with parchment. Spread the pecans on a rimmed baking sheet and toast just until fragrant, 7 to 8 minutes. Cool, then chop.

2. Whisk together the flour, cinnamon, salt, baking soda, nutmeg, and allspice in a bowl. Beat the sugar, brown sugar, eggs, oil, applesauce, and vanilla with an electric mixer on medium speed until combined, 45 seconds to 1 minute. Reduce the mixer speed to low and slowly add the flour mixture, scraping down sides of the bowl as needed. Fold in the apples and pecans. Divide the batter among the prepared pans. Bake until a toothpick inserted in the center comes out clean, 18 to 20 minutes. Cool in the pans on wire racks 5 minutes, then invert onto racks to cool completely.

3. Place 1 cake layer on a cake stand or serving platter and top with ¾ cup Salted Caramel Frosting. Repeat two more times. Frost the sides with the remaining frosting. Garnish with candied pecans.

SALTED CARAMEL
FROSTING

MAKES *3½ cups*
WORKING TIME *15 minutes*
TOTAL TIME *1 hour, 30 minutes*

- ¾ cup sugar
- ¾ cup heavy cream
- 2 teaspoons pure vanilla extract
- 1 cup (2 sticks) plus 2 tablespoons unsalted butter, at room temperature
- 1 teaspoon kosher salt
- 3 cups confectioners' sugar

1. Combine the sugar and 6 tablespoons of water in a small saucepan. Bring to a boil over medium-high heat and cook, without stirring, until the mixture turns a dark amber color, 10 to 12 minutes. Remove from the heat and slowly add the cream and vanilla, stirring with a wooden spoon until smooth. Cool 30 minutes.

2. Beat the butter and salt with an electric mixer on medium-high speed until light and fluffy, 3 to 4 minutes. Reduce the speed to low and slowly add the confectioners' sugar, scraping down the sides as needed. Slowly add the cooled caramel. Increase the speed to medium-high and beat until fluffy, 1 to 2 minutes. Refrigerate for 30 minutes.

CHRISTMAS TREE
SHEET CAKE

Colorful sprinkles in the batter give this cake a second helping of whimsy. Ornamental gumdrops, M&M's, and peppermint candies take shape around a caramel corn garland and a chocolate candy base on this classic sheet cake carved into the shape of a tree.

MAKES *12 to 16 servings*
WORKING TIME *1 hour, 30 minutes*
TOTAL TIME *3 hours*

Cooking spray

3⅓ cups cake flour, spooned and leveled

1½ tablespoons baking powder

¾ teaspoon kosher salt

1¾ cups milk

2 tablespoons fresh lemon juice

1 tablespoon pure vanilla extract

¾ cup (1½ sticks) unsalted butter, at room temperature

2¼ cups sugar

6 large egg whites

1 cup colored rainbow sprinkles

1 recipe White Vanilla Frosting (page 141)

2 tablespoons sifted unsweetened cocoa powder

40 drops green food coloring

Christmas Tree Template (countryliving.com/treecake)

Candy: yellow and red sour candy balls; mini white, red, and yellow M&M's; regular white, brown, and red M&M's; caramel popcorn; red gumdrops; peppermint hard candies; chocolate-covered raisins

1. Preheat the oven to 350°F. Spray a 9×13-inch baking pan with cooking spray and line with parchment paper.

2. Whisk together the flour, baking powder, and salt in a bowl. Stir together the milk, lemon juice, and vanilla in a separate bowl.

3. Beat the butter and sugar with an electric mixer on medium speed until fluffy, 1 to 2 minutes. Add the egg whites, one at a time, beating well after each addition. Reduce the mixer speed to low and beat in the flour mixture and milk mixture alternately, starting and ending with the flour mixture, just until incorporated. Stir in the sprinkles. Transfer the batter to the prepared pan; smooth the top.

4. Bake until a toothpick inserted in the center comes out clean, 40 to 50 minutes. Cool in the pan on a wire rack, 10 minutes, then invert onto the rack to cool completely.

5. Transfer ¾ cup of the frosting to a bowl. Add the cocoa powder and stir to combine. Dye the remaining frosting with green food coloring.

6. Place the template on the cake and cut the pieces with a long serrated knife along the outline.

7. Assemble the tree pieces on a serving platter, attaching them with a little green frosting, and frost them green. Assemble the stump, attaching the pieces with a little brown frosting, and frost them brown.

8. Create a star with yellow sour candy balls and mini M&M's. Create a garland with caramel popcorn, and decorate the tree with red gumdrops, red sour candy balls, mini white and red M&M's, regular white and red M&M's, and peppermint candies. Decorate the stump with brown M&M's and chocolate-covered raisins.

HOW TO
cut the tree

1 Print the template (countryliving.com/treecake) and cut out the pieces.

2 Cut the cake along the template using a long serrated knife.

3 Arrange the cake on a serving platter and frost.

4 Decorate!

photography credits

© **Jean Allsopp** 2, 37, 40 right, 41, 43, 48 right, 58, 80, 81, 87 top right, 98, 130, 201 top

© **Cedric Angeles** 10, 34, 62 top, 85, 92, 100 left, 128 right, 131 bottom right, 136, 191 right, 198 bottom

© **Burcu Avsar** cover (stockings), 12, 76, 142, 145, 146, 150, 154, 161, 162, 190, 196, 203 top left, 209 bottom right, 212 bottom

© **Mali Azima** 95, 112

© **Lincoln Barbour** 65

© **Susie Bell** 114, 134 right

© **Brown Bird Design** 247, 277 right, 283 right

© **Monica Buck** cover, 46, 47, 51, 53, 100 right, 195

© **Richard Burns** 127

© **Alun Callender** 198 top

© **Charlie Colmer** 9

© **Brent Darby** 20 right, 50, 109, 131 top,138, 177 bottom right, 179 left, 180 left, 193 left, 199, 200 bottom

© **Zach Desart** 67

© **Trevor Dixon** 32 top

© **Tara Donne** 87 top left

© **Sarah Dorio** 26, 32 bottom, 66, 75 bottom

© **Miki Duisterhof** 172, 176, 197, 212 right

© **Polly Eltes** 183, 186

© **Philip Ficks** 40 left

© **Tara Fisher** 169

© **Laurey W. Glenn** 87 bottom left

© **Catherine Gratwicke** 182

© **Melina Hammer** 152

© **David Hillegas** 1, 17, 22 right, 82, 119, 133, 136, 149, 170 left, 171, 177 bottom left, 192 bottom, 202, 208, 209 left and top right, 212 top left, back cover top left and right

© **Lisa Hubbard** 194 right

© **Jeremiah and Rachel Photography** 57

© **Max Kim-Bee** 16, 20 bottom, 48 left, 56, 61, 97, 107, 201 bottom, 203 bottom left

© **David Land** 13, 42, 54, 64 top, 86, 94, 193 right

© **Sarah Laye** 15

© **Living4Media/Thordis Ruggeberg** 204 top

© **Becky Luigart-Stayner** 55, 141, 165, 166, 271, 272, 275, 277 left, 278, 283 left, back cover bottom right

© **Randy Mayor** 4, 5, 8, 108, 213 right

© **Johnny Miller** 236, 243

© **Leslee Mitchell** 123, 213 left

© **Gareth Morgans** 250

© **Helen Norman** 70, 88, 93

© **Michael Partenio** 185

© **Victoria Pearson** 24, 33, 62 bottom, 99

© **Charlie Richards** 233, 249

© **Claire Richardson** 30, 178, 184 bottom, 187 right, 194 top

© **Lara Robby/Studio D** 174 left

© **Nassima Rothacker** 75, 128 left,

177 top right, 204 bottom, 205, 206, 207 right

© **Annie Schlechter** 19, 22 left, 23, 25, 36, 39, 49, 64 bottom, 68, 69, 90, 184 top, 200 top, 203 right

© **Victor A. Schrager** 174 right, 191 left

© **Mark Scott** 21, 84 left, 87 bottom right, 135 right

© **Christopher Shane** 14

Shutterstock 188 left

© **Seth Smoot** 117

© **Jody Stewart** 74

© **Buff Strickland** 35

© **Yuki Sugiura** 157, 258, 180 right

© **the ellaphant in the room** 44 left, 89

© **Debbie Treloar** 118

© **David Tsay** 6, 18, 28, 38, 52, 60, 63, 71, 72, 73, 96, 101, 102, 103, 104, 105, 106

courtesy of **Wikimedia Foundation** 129 bottom

© **Anna Williams** 192 top

© **Clare Winfield** 84 right

© **Rachel Whiting** 110, 113, 129 top, 132, 134 left, 135 left, 137, 175, 178, 194 left, 207 left, 214, 215

© **Brian Woodcock** 29, 44 right, 78, 115, 116, 120, 122, 124, 125, 126 right, 131 bottom left, 148, 170 right, 179 right, 187 left, 188 right, 189, 210, 217, 218, 220, 222, 231, 234, 238, 241, 244, 252, 254, 259, 260, 261, 263, 266, 281, back cover

287

HEARSTBOOKS

An Imprint of Sterling Publishing Co., Inc.
1166 Avenue of the Americas
New York, NY 10036

HEARST BOOKS and COUNTRY LIVING are registered trademarks and
the distinctive Hearst Books logo is a trademark of Hearst Communications, Inc.

© 2018 Hearst Communications, Inc.

ISBN 978-1-61837-270-3

Hearst Communications, Inc. has made every effort to ensure that all information in this publication is accurate.
However, due to differing conditions, tools, and individual skills, Hearst Communications, Inc. cannot be responsible
for any injuries, losses, and/or damages that may result from the use of any information in this publication.

Distributed in Canada by Sterling Publishing
c/o Canadian Manda Group, 664 Annette Street
Toronto, Ontario M6S 2C8, Canada
Distributed in Australia by NewSouth Books
45 Beach Street, Coogee, NSW 2034, Australia

For information about custom editions, special sales, and premium and corporate purchases,
please contact Sterling Special Sales at 800-805-5489 or specialsales@sterlingpublishing.com.

Manufactured in China

2 4 6 8 10 9 7 5 3 1

sterlingpublishing.com
countryliving.com

Cover design by Nancy Singer & woolypear
Interior design by woolypear
Photography credits on page 287